POLICY AND PRACTICE IN E

NUMBER TEN

GAELIC MEDIUM EDUCATION

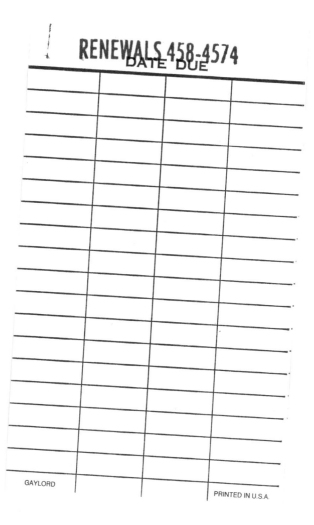

POLICY AND PRACTICE IN EDUCATION

POLICY AND PRACTICE IN EDUCATION

EDITORS

GORDON KIRK *AND* ROBERT GLAISTER

GAELIC MEDIUM EDUCATION

Edited by

Margaret Nicolson and Matthew MacIver

Contributors

**D. J. MacLeod, Wilson McLeod, Jean Nisbet
and Rosemary Ward**

DUNEDIN ACADEMIC PRESS

EDINBURGH

Published by
Dunedin Academic Press Ltd
Hudson House
8 Albany Street
Edinburgh EH1 3QB
Scotland

ISBN 1 903765 34 X
ISSN 1479-6910

British Library Cataloguing in Publication Data
A catalogue record for this book is available from the British Library

Typeset by Patty Rennie Production, Portsoy
Printed in Great Britain by Cromwell Press

CONTENTS

SERIES EDITORS' INTRODUCTION

Education is now widely regarded as having a key contribution to make to national prosperity and to the well-being of the community. Arguably, of all forms of investment in the public good, it deserves the highest priority. Given the importance of education, it is natural that it should be the focus of widespread public interest and that the effectiveness and responsiveness of the educational service should be of vital concern to politicians, teachers and other professionals, parents and members of the general public. If anything, the establishment of Scotland's parliament, which has already affirmed education as a key priority, will witness an intensification of public interest in the nature and direction of educational policy and the changing practices in the schools. This series of books on *Policy and Practice in Education* seeks to support the public and professional discussion of education in Scotland.

In recent years there have been significant changes in every aspect of education in Scotland. The series seeks to counter the tendency for such changes to be under-documented and to take place without sufficient critical scrutiny. While it will focus on changes of policy and practice in Scotland, it will seek to relate developments to the wider international debate on education.

Each volume in the series will focus on a particular aspect of education, reflecting upon the past, analysing the present, and contemplating the future. The contributing authors are all well established and bring to their writing an intimate knowledge of their field, as well as the capacity to offer a readable and authoritative analysis of policies and practices.

The coordinators of this volume, the 10th in the series, are Margaret Nicolson, Senior Lecturer and Staff Tutor in Languages, with the Open University in Scotland and Matt MacIver, Chief Executive and Registrar, the General Teaching Council (Scotland).

Professor Gordon Kirk
Vice-Principal
The University of Edinburgh

Dr Robert T D Glaister
Faculty of Education
and Language Studies
The Open University in Scotland

EDITORIAL INTRODUCTION

This volume has been undertaken with three main objectives in mind. First of all it aims to bring the subject of Gaelic Medium Education (GME) to a wider audience than may have previously known about it, thus allowing for a more widespread and informed debate on the subject. Secondly, in line with the title of this series, it aims to create a marriage between points of policy and practice so that the divide, often artificially created between these two in much of Scotland's educational history, may be filled to some extent. Thirdly, it aims to increase general awareness about issues of language, often neglected in a monolingual world.

Our grateful thanks go the chapter authors who practise in or advise and write on Gaelic Medium Education and on languages more generally in the Scottish context. D. J. MacLeod has always worked in Gaelic education and is currently responsible for co-ordinating the development of GME in Highland Council. His chapter traces the historical development of GME and surveys its current position. Wilson McLeod is a lecturer in Celtic and Scottish Studies at the University of Edinburgh and was formerly the Course Leader in Gaelic with North Atlantic Studies at Sabhal Mòr Ostaig. In chapter two he examines minority language-medium education in the Basque country, Wales and Ireland, offering a point of comparison against which to measure the development of GME in Scotland. Rosemary Ward has been involved in teaching and developing Gaelic Medium Education since 1986 and is currently a Quality Improvement Officer for Argyll and Bute Education Service. In her chapter she writes from the practitioner's perspective, focusing on the challenges which affect staff working in GME in schools. Jean Nisbet is Quality Improvement Officer with East Ayrshire Council. In chapter four she discusses the role of local authorities in the GME debate and in its delivery. In Chapter 5 we examine the educational, linguistic and political contexts in Scotland, all of which impact upon GME, and suggest some issues which will require attention if GME is to thrive.

Our thanks also go to those, too numerous to mention, who have provided invaluable information, advice and support along the way. We are particularly indebted to Dunedin Academic Press for their commitment to the subject.

Margaret Nicolson and Matthew MacIver
March 2003

GLOSSARY

BAC	Basque Autonomous Community Three of the four Basque provinces in Spain make up the Basque Autonomous Community which contains some 75% of the total Basque population
Bòrd na Gàidhlig	The Gaelic Board The Gaelic Board set up by the Scottish Executive in 2000
Bunsgoil Ghàidhlig Ghlaschu	The Gaelic School Glasgow
CCG	Comataidh Craolaidh Gàidhlig Gaelic Broadcasting Committee
CLI-na Gaidheil Ura	The Gaelic Learners' Association
CNAG	Comunn na Gàidhlig
CNE — CNES	Comhairle nan Eilean (Western Isles Council) later renamed Comhairle nan Eilean Siar
CNSA	Comhairle nan Sgoiltean Araich The Gaelic Nursery Schools Association
COSLA	Convention of Scottish Local Authorities
CNP	Comunn nam Pàrant The Parents Association — sometimes referred to as Nàiseanta, ie The National Parents Association
Croileagan	Gaelic Playgroups
GLPS	Gaelic Language in the Primary School
GME	Gaelic Medium Education

GMU	Gaelic Medium Units
GTCS	General Teaching Council for Scotland
HMIE	Her Majesty's Inspectors of Education
IASG	Inter-authority Steering Group
MLPS	Modern Languages in the Primary School
MRG	Inter-authority Management Review Group
PRG	Inter-authority Primary Review Group
PGCE	Post Graduate Certificate in Education
SRG	Inter-authority Secondary Review Groups
SEED	Scottish Executive Education Department
SMO	Sabhal Mòr Ostaig
UHIMI	University of the Highlands and Islands Millennium Institute
TEI	Teacher Education Institution

CHAPTER 1

AN HISTORICAL OVERVIEW

D. J. MacLeod

Introduction

This chapter aims to give an historical overview of the development of Gaelic Medium Education and of policy related to its implementation from the Education Act in 1872 to the present day, in order to create a better understanding of how it has reached its current position within the Scottish education system. It will also discuss some of the issues which have marked GME's development over that period.

The Background

The 1872 Education Act, which introduced universal schooling in Scotland, did not mention Gaelic let alone the concept of teaching through the medium of Gaelic. Some of the new schools nevertheless taught Gaelic as a subject and in 1905 a Leaving Certificate in Gaelic at the Lower grade was introduced with a Higher Paper in Gaelic following in 1916. Gaelic was recognised as part of the official curriculum in Scottish schools with the Gaelic clause of the 1918 Education Act, but this recognition was limited as only education authorities in Gaelic-speaking areas were obliged to make provision for Gaelic and this applied only to the teaching of Gaelic as a subject.

Gaelic was little used, then or for long after, as the medium of teaching in schools, even in strongly Gaelic areas. Indeed Gaelic language and literature were usually taught through the medium of English. This created in the minds of many generations of Gaelic speakers an inescapable association between the English language and education which it has proved very difficult to change.

The first systematic attempt to introduce Gaelic as the language of the classroom was the Inverness-shire Gaelic Education Scheme, which was launched in Skye and the Inverness-shire Outer Isles (Barra, the Uists and

Harris) in 1960. The principal aim of this programme was 'to provide for the Gaelic-speaking pupil a fuller and more appropriate education by making as much use as is reasonable of his mother tongue' (MacLeod, 1966, p.326). Even this modest attempt to change the established practice, and the attitudes it had given rise to, ran into opposition at first, the Council's Gaelic Supervisor, Murdo Macleod, reporting in 1963 that the use of Gaelic as a teaching medium was 'proving difficult to effect' (MacLeod, 1966, p.332).

However, Inverness-shire Council persisted with the Scheme, targeting the new curricular area of Environmental Studies, topic-based work covering a range of subjects and developed in response to the 1965 *Primary Memorandum* (SOED, 1965). This proved a wise choice because Environmental Studies was new and flexible and, by its nature, exploited links between schools and their environment and community. By 1968, when Macleod left Inverness-shire Council, the situation was much more encouraging than had been the case five years earlier.

The Inverness-shire Scheme represents a significant step along the road to GME but, since it was a voluntary scheme, its success was restricted to schools which happened to have enthusiastic teachers. It had lost some of its momentum by the time the next step forward came in 1975.

When Comhairle nan Eilean (the Western Isles Council) came into being in that year, one of its first actions was to set up a Bilingual Education Project, the aim of which was to devise 'situations and activities which stimulate children to use Gaelic as a natural language for the exploration and description of experience' (Murray and Morrison, 1984, p.5). The Project started with 20 schools, expanding to 34 three years later, and in 1981 it was re-constituted as the Bilingual Curriculum Development Unit, taking in all 54 island primary schools. In 1983, the scheme was extended, on a pilot basis, to the secondary sector when two secondary schools, Lionel and Shawbost in Lewis, began teaching History and Geography in Gaelic to pupils who had come through the bilingual project.

The Bilingual Project gained a deserved international reputation for its success in encouraging schools to devise a curriculum rooted in the local community, since it too concentrated on Environmental Studies, and for its more child-centred approach. However, its other main objective, to introduce Gaelic gradually alongside English as a medium of teaching, was less uniformly successful. It is now clear in fact that the term 'bilingual education' in this context covered a wide variety of practices, ranging from innovative inter-play between the two languages to teaching which was bilingual in little more than name.

In retrospect, it was perhaps unrealistic to expect that the generations-old tradition of teaching through the medium of English could be changed through a bilingual approach which did not specify the proportion of time to be devoted to each language and relied largely on encouragement and example. Experience elsewhere has shown that where one language is much stronger than the other — in this case the teachers themselves had been taught and trained in English and had access to much better resources in that language — there is almost always a gradual drift in favour of the majority language.

In any event, the demographic context in which the Project operated was changing. The Project had aimed to provide bilingual education for bilingual children but more and more non-Gaelic speaking children were entering the schools by this time and the Project's approach proved less well equipped to cope with this development. Not only did these children not learn Gaelic but the parents of native Gaelic-speaking children were often heard to complain that their children had 'lost their Gaelic' when they went to school. Television, pop music and peer pressure all played a part in influencing children to switch from Gaelic to English as their language of choice. But the school system has to share the blame in the sense that the bilingual approach did not provide a strong enough counter-balance to these other influences. This is borne out by the National Census figures which show that, in the area covered by the Western Isles Bilingual Project, the number of 5–15 year olds speaking Gaelic fell from 3,978 (70% of the peer group) in 1981 to 2,302 (or 51%) ten years later, an alarming fall of 42%.

Gaelic Medium Pre-school Education

By the early 1980s it was becoming clear to most observers that the decline of Gaelic had entered a critical phase throughout Scotland and that the situation was especially serious in the language's erstwhile heartland of the Western Isles. It was also becoming clear to many that education was a factor, among others, in that decline and, by the same token, that education could be one element in trying to arrest the process. While a fatalistic attitude to the decline of Gaelic was emerging in some quarters, there were some who refused to accept this. They took their inspiration from Wales.

By the 1980s Welsh-medium education had been operating for some forty years and was seen to be producing new generations of Welsh speakers, not only arresting the decline of the language but restoring it to areas where it had died out. While the Western Isles Bilingual Project had looked for inspiration to the 'natural Welsh schools' of strongly Welsh North Wales, in the 1980s a new brand of Gaelic activist started to visit anglicised South Wales, coming back fired with enthusiasm for the new 'total immersion' approach that they had witnessed there. Their message was met with some scepticism at first but, gradually, it gained ground and the first Gaelic-medium parent-run playgroups began to appear. After a short-lived experiment in Inverness in the 1970s, four Gaelic playgroups were set up in 1980–81 in Oban, Edinburgh, Pitlochry and Sleat (Skye), and on May 15th 1982 an important step was taken at the first meeting of the four groups when a support organisation, Comhairle nan Sgoitteara Araich, (CNSA), was set up.

CNSA's main objective was the survival of the Gaelic language. This has been a weakness in some respects. Some commentators have referred to a perceived lack of educational expertise, for example, and to the quality of the support provided [SOED, 1994], but it was precisely this clear focus on language which helped make the movement so effective at the outset. In particular it struck a chord with parents who were becoming extremely concerned about the future of Gaelic. These parents responded positively to the CNSA initiative. The number of Gaelic playgroups, starting with four in 1982, doubled in the following year and continued to increase rapidly, throughout Scotland until 1994 when it hit a peak of 148 groups and 2,620 children.

The rapid growth of Gaelic playgroups was partly a result of the lack of local authority nursery provision at that time. The first Gaelic-medium nursery class was set up by the Highland Regional Council in Inverness in 1988. Nursery classes in Portree and Edinburgh soon followed but this sector took off only after the government introduced a policy of nursery education for all three- and four-year olds in 1997. Most authorities now provide Gaelic-medium pre-school education in support of Gaelic-medium primary classes: there were 36 nursery classes with around 500 children in 2001. This development has obvious implications for CNSA's future role, which it is currently striving to address.

CNSA's Gaelic playgroups (and the local authority nursery classes) are open to both Gaelic-speaking children and children from homes where Gaelic is not spoken. In most mainland groups membership is drawn mainly from the latter category. CNSA's policy is an all-Gaelic one. Immersed in the language from an early age, children from homes where Gaelic is not spoken are soon able to understand the Gaelic spoken to them in the playgroup and, by the time they leave it, have started speaking Gaelic.

Gaelic Medium School Education

Those behind the playgroups had always recognised, however, that these groups by themselves would not save the language. GME in schools was essential if children from non-Gaelic speaking backgrounds were to acquire the language fully. As a result, groups of parents who had been involved in running Gaelic playgroups soon began to ask their local authorities to provide Gaelic-medium primary school classes for their children. The leaders in these mostly informal groups were professional people, themselves often involved in Gaelic education, usually knowledgeable about language and confident enough to take the first steps into what was, in Scotland, largely unknown territory at this time. Initially there was some opposition on the part of the local authorities. While institutionalised prejudice against Gaelic may have been a factor, some education officials were also genuinely concerned about the implications of educating children through a language other than that of the home. This is widely accepted internationally, for example in Wales, Ireland, Catalunya, Friesland and Canada, but was little known in Scotland at this time. Once the political decisions had been taken to proceed, to their credit, the officers who had been sceptical at the outset did their best to make the development work.

The first designated Gaelic-medium primary classes to be set up in Scotland in 1985 were in the Sir John Maxwell Primary in Glasgow and the Central School, Inverness. Central started with a small P1 class and Sir John Maxwell with P1 to P5, the total roll in these classes being 24 at the start. A bilingual P1 class was set up in Portree in the same year, and this became a Gaelic-medium P1/2 class in 1986. 1986 also saw the first Gaelic-medium class set up in the Western Isles, in Breasclete, Lewis.

Gaelic-medium primary education was ready to take off. That process was assisted by the launch of a new organisation, Comunn na Gàidhlig, (CNAG), in 1984. It had been set up primarily to co-ordinate activities related to Gaelic but also to initiate developments where there were gaps. It played an important facilitating role in the early years of GME, encouraging hesitant parents to apply for it and then liaising with the authorities on their behalf.

Another important catalyst was the creation in 1986 by the Scottish Office, with the consent of the Convention of Scottish Local Authorities, (COSLA), of the Gaelic Specific Grants Scheme, Specific Grants being a means whereby central government channels revenue support towards special developments run by local authorities. Specific Grants meant that the authorities could set up Gaelic classes without compromising their existing educational provision which, politically, was a key point.

From a starting average of two new classes each year, the movement gathered momentum, rising to six between 1989 and 1993, before slowing down again to three a year between 1994 and 1999. The number of pupils involved has increased steadily, reaching a peak of 1,928 in 2002, with roughly a third each in Highland, Western Isles and the Lowlands.

In line with the playgroups, Gaelic-medium primary classes are open to children with Gaelic and to children from homes where Gaelic is not spoken. The latter are usually in the majority, especially in mainland schools. Gaelic is the language of teaching for most, usually all, of the time: this is referred to as 'immersion' or 'total immersion'. This approach provides ideal conditions for language teaching, namely a strong incentive to learn the language in order to participate in the work of the class, extensive exposure to it and the opportunity to use the language for meaningful purposes while learning it. This, coupled with children's ability to assimilate at that age, means that GME pupils from homes where Gaelic is not spoken soon become competent users of Gaelic. It has also meant that native-speaking children are usually more likely to want to continue speaking Gaelic, despite the complaints of some parents that Gaelic-medium classes are geared more towards the needs of children who are not native speakers.

The first Gaelic-medium teachers were Gaelic speakers who transferred from English-medium teaching. Subsequently, new teachers qualified in the primary sector and native Gaelic speakers were recruited straight from the colleges, resulting in a current younger than average teaching cohort. In some centres trainee teachers have been able to take optional courses in Gaelic-medium methodology, although there is as yet no dedicated Gaelic-medium teacher training course.

Although there have been a few minor setbacks — two small primary classes closed down, for example — Gaelic-medium primary education has been an almost unqualified success, with school rolls rising steadily if not dramatically in some cases. The main problems have been those associated with such rapid success, such as a shortage of teachers to meet the demand.

However, the growth of GME has hit a plateau in recent years. There have been no new units established in the last three years and the overall numbers have not increased significantly. There are several reasons for this. The main one is the shortage of Gaelic-speaking teachers. Several proposed new classes have failed to start because teachers could not be found and, generally, this lack has affected parental and local authority confidence. Another reason is that in many areas the initial demand has now been met: in many parts of the West Highlands and the Islands, for example, most families now have access to GME within reasonable travelling distance. The fact that school rolls generally are falling throughout Scotland, and especially in country areas, is also a factor.

In 1988, the first pupils to come through Gaelic-medium primary education in Glasgow moved on to Hillpark Secondary School in the city. The growth of Gaelic-medium secondary education has been dependent on the availability of Gaelic-speaking subject teachers and, as a result, progress has been uneven. The Scottish Office report of 1994 concluded that 'the provision of Gaelic-medium secondary education in a number of subjects, determined by the vagaries of resource availability, is neither desirable nor feasible in the foreseeable future' (SOED, 1994, p.3). The Scottish Office was later to change its stance in the face of concerted opposition from local authorities, Gaelic organisations and parents' groups, and GME has continued in the secondary sector. However, it is still subject to the original constraints and the level of provision is still unsatisfactory.

In 2001/2002, for example, of the 32 secondary schools receiving pupils from Gaelic-medium primary classes, all provided a Gaelic language class (for a total of 928 pupils), but only 14 offered any subject teaching through the medium of Gaelic and only 302 pupils, or a third of the total, benefitted from this. While two schools, in Portree and Stornoway, offered a range of subjects in Gaelic, most provided only one or two.

Emerging Policy

Although the rapid growth of GME took most local authorities by surprise at first, many quickly accepted it as an established part of their educational provision and began to put in place policies and structures to regulate and support it.

While not all authorities have a formal policy for setting up Gaelic-medium classes, the practice in most is broadly similar, namely to react positively to demand from parents, subject to certain practical conditions such as availability of accommodation, funding and staff, and viable class sizes (usually around 4 pupils each year). Gaelic organisations and parents' groups have campaigned for parents to have a statutory right to GME but this has not yet been granted and COSLA, responding on behalf of the local authorities to a government consultation exercise in 1997, expressed its opposition to 'the imposition of a duty to provide Gaelic medium education' (COSLA, 1997). However the Standards in Scottish Schools Act of 2000 recognised Gaelic education as a National Priority, requiring authorities to indicate their plans for its development, and due account is taken of GME in national curricular initiatives, such as Higher Still and the 5–14 Development Programme.

Local authority policy on the balance of the languages varies, with Highland and Western Isles (now known as CNES) representing the two ends of the spectrum. In Highland, Gaelic is the spoken medium of teaching at all stages from nursery through to primary 7 and for all aspects of the curriculum including Maths, Science and English Language, although pupils read and write in both Gaelic and English from primary 3 [Highland Council, 2000]. In CNES schools, according to its Bilingual Education Policy Implementation Review, Gaelic-medium pupils 'are taught entirely in Gaelic up to primary 2', 'oral English is introduced in the third year', in primary 4 'the principal targets in mathematics [are] also dealt with through the medium of English' and by primary 6 and 7 'a balanced bilingual approach [permeates] the curriculum'. (CNES, 1996, pp.3–4) As more children from homes where Gaelic is not spoken enter GME in the Western Isles, it will be interesting to see if there is the same drift towards the dominant language as happened in previous bilingual programmes. The Council's expectation is that the early total immersion phase will safeguard against this eventuality.

Schools in other areas are all somewhere on this spectrum, with those in English-speaking areas more likely to use Gaelic as the medium of teaching rather than adopting a bilingual approach, in an effort to counterbalance the dominance of English in pupils' home and community life.

Organisationally, it is the policy of most authorities to provide Gaelic-medium primary education through separate classes within otherwise English-medium schools. In the Western Isles, however, all Gaelic-medium pupils are taught separately until P2 but thereafter may either form a separate Gaelic-medium track, referred to as the 'twin track' approach, or may join their counterparts in the designated 'bilingual' section of the school.

The only free-standing Gaelic-medium primary school is Bunsgoil Ghàidhlig Ghlaschu, set up in Glasgow in 1999. The Highland Council has agreed to build a new Gaelic school in Inverness and there has been pressure elsewhere for similar provision, notably in Edinburgh. CNES has designated four small rural schools as 'Gaelic-medium schools': these are schools with a majority of Gaelic-medium pupils but each also has a small English-medium department, making them in practice dual-medium schools.

Support Infrastructure

A support infrastructure for GME has evolved, albeit somewhat unevenly, over the years. The authorities with a significant number of Gaelic-medium classes, Highland, Western Isles and Strathclyde (later Argyll and Bute), set up resource centres and appointed support staff in the early years, although much of this structure has been eroded. In authorities with only one or two schools involved in GME there has been less support. Specialist back-up for Gaelic-medium education is patchy: some authorities have Gaelic-speaking Support for Learning teachers but many do not and the number of Gaelic-speaking educational psychologists and speech therapists is very limited.

Gaelic teaching materials were in extremely short supply, and often of a poor quality, when GME started in the mid-1980s. In order to tackle this problem the local authorities involved set up inter-authority projects which were 75% funded by Gaelic Specific Grant and managed by inter-authority working groups. The two groups most directly involved in resources production were the advisorate-level Primary and Secondary Review Groups (PRG and SRG). Between 1986 and 1999, PRG and SRG produced a large quantity of high-quality materials covering all aspects of the curriculum, primary and secondary. Most of the projects were managed by officials from a small number of authorities, Western Isles, Highland and Argyll and Bute in particular. This work has now been taken over by the National Gaelic Resources Centre, Storlann Naiseanta na Gàidhlig, which was set up by SEED in 1999 and which also aims to support schools in other appropriate ways.

PRG also ran annual national conferences of Gaelic primary teachers in the early years, which helped to give the movement direction at a formative stage. SEED organised a national seminar for Gaelic-medium primary teachers in November 2002 as a prelude to setting up a network of Gaelic-medium teachers, to be known as 'A' Chuisle'.

Shortage of Gaelic-speaking primary teachers has been the main constraint on the development of GME. Various promotional campaigns and local and national governmental interventions have been launched over the years, aimed at increasing the supply of Gaelic-speaking teachers. These have resulted in a marked increase in teacher numbers but GME has continued to grow at an even faster rate and, as a result, the supply of Gaelic-medium teachers, currently running at around 15/20 primary and 3/5 secondary teachers each year, is still not usually enough to meet the demand.

Although optional modules on GME are part of some teacher education courses, there is as yet no dedicated Gaelic-medium course, despite a strong recommendation to that effect in the 1999 General Teaching Council report on the subject. Besides, the courses are still delivered largely in Aberdeen and Glasgow, compounding the difficulties experienced by schools in rural areas in recruiting Gaelic teachers. These difficulties are now being addressed.

University Celtic Departments, contrary to the situation in minority language contexts elsewhere such as Wales, Ireland or Friesland, have not played a significant role in the development of GME, producing few new Gaelic-medium teachers, for example, and little directly applicable research. Most of the latter has been commissioned by the local authorities. This has occasionally involved university Celtic Departments in applied research, producing children's dictionaries and grammar books, for example, but the authorities have mostly worked with the independent research agency, Lèirsinn, which has produced reports for them on various aspects of GME. The private agency, Sgrùd, through its demographic analyses and surveys, has also played a useful role in informing the development of Gaelic education policy.

Sabhal Mor Ostaig has been a particular source of inspiration to those involved in GME in the Further and Higher Education sectors. Starting as a Gaelic-medium Further Education college specialising in Business Studies, its first full-time course started in 1983; it has since branched out into other subject areas and recently started offering degree courses as a constituent college of the UHI-Millennium Institute.

Gaelic parents' groups have been the mainstay of GME. In the early days these were mostly informal groups, centred on one or two enthusiasts. Several local branches of a new organisation, Comunn nam Pàrant, (CNP), were set up as early as 1984. When CNP was launched as a national organisation in 1994, with a fulltime development officer, it began to play a more significant role.

The main function of CNP is to represent the parents of Gaelic-medium pupils at a national level and in particular to lobby politicians and others in authority on their behalf. It has also played an educative role, running national seminars on aspects of GME, for example. There are also local branches of CNP, whose main role is to represent Gaelic-medium parents at a school level, although some also take part in activities such as fund-raising and publicity. Many have often found it hard to carve out a niche for themselves alongside the various parents' groups already in existence. Seen by many schools as chiefly political pressure groups, they have sometimes found it difficult to establish the comfortable working relationship with school managements which parent-teacher associations usually enjoy.

The areas of GME where most support is still needed are the family and neighbourhood. Many Gaelic-medium pupils live in homes and communities in which they have little contact with Gaelic. This is likely to affect their perception of the value and relevance of the language, as well as limiting their opportunities to develop their competence through wide-ranging use of the language.

This problem is more a matter for the wider Gaelic community, including parents' groups and the appropriate Gaelic organisations, than for the school authorities. Nonetheless, some of the latter have become involved. One authority (Highland) provides an integrated support programme through its Community Learning and Leisure Service, comprising information days, workshops, Gaelic classes and a library service for parents and, for pupils, after-school clubs, activities and an annual week-long 'residential school' (in which pupils spend a week in a centre with their teachers, taking part in a programme of educational, social and recreational events).

Despite these developments, it would be fair to say that the problem has yet to be tackled in a systematic way. Books, TV programmes, CDs, and computer software for leisure use are in very limited supply, if they exist at all. The Sradagan junior clubs, set up by CNAG in 1986, serve a useful function but, apart from some one-off events, there is little for teenagers. Feisean, a gathering of young people where they learn traditional music and culture, are attractive to youngsters but only two are conducted through Gaelic. Schools sometimes perceive parents, rightly or wrongly, as not doing enough to support their efforts by learning Gaelic or speaking it to their children. Overall, much clearly remains to be done.

Evaluation

Many people, not least the parents involved, take a keen interest in the educational progress of pupils in GME. Local authority quality improvement departments and the Inspectorate monitor attainment in Gaelic-medium classes with at least as much rigour as English-medium education. In addition, in 1995 the Scottish Office commissioned Stirling University to lead a major multi-agency research project into the attainments of pupils in Gaelic-medium primary education. Their report, published in 1999, concluded that 'pupils receiving Gaelic-medium primary education . . . were not being disadvantaged in comparison with children educated through English. In many, though not all, instances they outperformed English-medium pupils and, in addition, gained the advantage of having become proficient in two languages.' (Johnstone, 1999, p.4)

In terms of progress in Gaelic, the Gaelic 5/14 Report stated that Gaelic-medium pupils should be 'at the stage of broadly equal competence in Gaelic and English, in all skills, by the end of Primary 7' (Scottish Office Education Department, 1993, p.6). Experience has shown that most do achieve this target, although their English writing is often slightly better than their Gaelic. In particular, they are usually able to communicate in an easy, uninhibited way in Gaelic by primary 7, though usually not yet with native-speaker fluency, before going on to develop their accuracy and range in Gaelic in the secondary school.

Wider Implications

And what, finally, is the effect of these developments on the prospects for the survival of Gaelic? The evidence is mixed. In the crucial Western Isles area the picture is not encouraging. The proportion of children in Gaelic-medium primary education there in 2002/3 was only 25%. Even allowing for the fact that not all Gaelic-speaking children are in Gaelic-medium classes, this figure compares unfavourably with the 51% of Western Isles 5–15 year olds who were Gaelic-speaking in 1991. The overall total of Gaelic speakers in this area fell by 19.6% between 1991 and 2001. That reduction is a matter of grave concern, for if Gaelic loses its heartland, its survival elsewhere will be a somewhat artificial one.

There are more encouraging figures from areas with a strong Gaelic tradition but where Gaelic is no longer a community language. In Portree, for example, 45% of primary school children were being taught through Gaelic in 2003 and the figure for the whole of Skye was 30%. These figures indicate that GME is beginning to slow the decline of Gaelic in such areas. In addition, new Gaelic speakers are being created in urban areas in the Lowlands, with around 1,200 at all stages in 2003.

Nationally, the current annual throughput of GME is around 300, while recent census returns show the number of Gaelic speakers falling by an average of 700 each year. If that trend continues, the number of Gaelic speakers might be expected to fall for several more decades, stabilising eventually at about 25,000. If, on the other hand, the trend is to be reversed, the number of children acquiring the language must increase around two- or three-fold. Since inter-generational transmission has declined to a trickle, a new phase of growth will be required in GME, surpassing what has gone before.

How feasible is this expectation? Experience suggests that there is a latent demand for GME in many areas which active encouragement would bring to the fore. Those responsible for promoting and providing GME have been reluctant to provide such encouragement in recent years because of the teacher supply situation but, if this problem could be resolved, the situation could be transformed.

In summary, the position regarding the use of Gaelic in schools education in Scotland has been dramatically turned on its head since the first half of last century. Then, native Gaelic-speaking pupils in strongly Gaelic communities were taught Gaelic through the medium of English and education was undoubtedly a factor in the language's decline. Now most of the pupils in GME come from non-Gaelic-speaking homes and communities and the school is, in effect, the main hope for the survival of the language. In the process, many problems have been encountered and many solutions, some ingenious, have evolved. There are clear lessons to be learned from this process that extend much further than the Gaelic world and have implications especially for language teaching in Scotland. The wider educational and political issues are also apparent and will be developed later in this volume.

Table 1: Gaelic-medium primary classes

Year	New classes: Schools	Authority	New classes	Total	Pupils
1985	Central (Inverness) Sir John Maxwell (Glasgow)	Highland Strathclyde	2	2	24
1986	Portree Breasclete	Highland Western Isles	2	4	64
1987	Broadford, Sleat, Craighill (Tain) Stoneybridge (Uist) Bowmore	Highland Western Isles Strathclyde	5	8	112
1988	Staffin Meadowburn (Bishopbriggs) Tollcross (Edinburgh)	Highland Strathclyde Lothian	3	12	169
1989	Back, Iochdar, Carinish, Shawbost, Stornoway Cornaigmore (Tiree)	Western Isles Strathclyde	6	18	286
1990	Gairloch, Newtonmore, Dunvegan, Plockton Aird (Point, Lewis), Barvas, Daliburgh, Bayble	Highland Western Isles	8	26	431
1991	Laxdale, Tarbert, Balivanich South Lodge (Invergordon) Gilcomstoun (Aberdeen)	Western Isles Highland Grampian	5	31	614
1992	Leverburgh, Castlebay, Carloway Dingwall, Acharacle, Lochcarron Mount Cameron (East Kilbride)	Western Isles Highland Strathclyde	7	38	824
1993	Lady Lovat, Ullapool, Tongue Airidhantuim, Uig (Lewis), Knockanduie/Balallan Northern District/Goodlyburn (Perth)	Highland Western Isles Tayside	7	45	1080
1994	Fort William RC Lionel Dales Park (Peterhead)	Highland Western Isles Grampian	3	47	1260
1995	Bernera, Dunskellar Kirkriggs (Forfar)	Western Isles Angus	3	50	1456
1996	Salen Kilmuir Sandwick	Argyll & Bute Highland Western Isles	3	52	1587
1997	Oban Onthank (Kilmarnock) Condorrat	Argyll & Bute East Ayrshire North Lanarkshire	3	55	1736

1998	Riverside (Stirling)	Stirling	1	56	1816
1999	Eriskay Sandbank (Dunoon) Highlander Academy (Greenock)	Western Isles Argyll & Bute Inverclyde	3	59	1831
2000			—	59	1862
2001			—	59	1859

Table 2: Gaelic-medium pre-school provision

Year	Playgroups	Children	Nurseries	Pupils	Total pupils
1982	4	40			
1983	8	75			
1984	14	170			
1985	26	270			
1986	38	500			
1987	49	660			
1988	63	920	1	[Figures not available]	
1989	74	1200	2	[Figures not available]	
1990	83	1420	3	30	1450
1991	99	1710	3	54	1764
1992	122	2065	3	69	2134
1993	142	2480	3	54	2480
1994	148	2620	3	74	2694
1995	141	2510	3	66	2576
1996	144	2550	3	59	2609
1997	145	2416	10	134*	2550*
1998	120	1830	24	211*	2041*
1999	[Figures not available]		33	276*	—
2000	129	1850	34	413*	2263*
2001			36	403*	

The nursery figures are for the start of the school year: children enter local authority pre-school provision at several points through the year as they attain the appropriate age.

CHAPTER 2

GAELIC MEDIUM EDUCATION IN THE INTERNATIONAL CONTEXT

Wilson McLeod

Since the 1970s minority-language education has developed rapidly in a number of countries and communities throughout Europe and beyond, from Saami in Scandinavia to Maori in New Zealand. GME in Scotland has derived inspiration, guidance and expertise from this international experience. Indeed, Scotland is by no means at the forefront, for other countries have taken minority-language education much further and have achieved striking successes in institutionalising once-excluded minority languages in their education systems, on a scale much greater than anything seen in Scotland, even in the strongest Gaelic-speaking areas. Two of the most remarkable success stories are Wales and the Basque Country, specifically the Basque Autonomous Community, (BAC), where Welsh and Basque have developed new vigour as a result of focused educational policy. In different ways, Irish-medium education has also grown rapidly in Ireland, both North and South, in recent years. This chapter will review the Welsh, Basque and Irish experiences from a Scottish Gaelic perspective, highlighting the possible lessons for Gaelic educationalists and policy-makers in Scotland.

The 'gentle revolution' in Welsh-medium education (Baker 1993) shows Gaelic educationalists and activists what can be achieved in terms of institutionalising minority-language education through systematic, incremental progress over the course of many years. The case of Wales has direct relevance for Scotland in that these successes have been secured within a different part of the same state (albeit distinct in relation to administration and educational structures) and within a highly similar political and administrative environment and ethos. The Basque Country is quite different from Scotland in terms of its history during the twentieth century, but the rapid development of Basque education from a position in the 1960s far less favourable than that of Gaelic demonstrates the results that are possible in a short space of time given serious institutional and community commitment. There are necessarily limits to any comparison of this kind. Both Welsh and Basque are considerably more widely spoken than Gaelic (at the most recent censuses, 2001 for Wales and Scotland and 1996 for the Basque country, there were some 580,000 Welsh speakers in Wales (20.5% of the population) and some 625,000 Basque speakers in the Basque Country (30.9%) compared to some 58,000 Gaelic speakers in Scotland (1.2%)). More important, the political contexts are quite different: where Welsh and Basque are unquestionably perceived as national languages, as badges of national identity, and draw great strength from those national(ist) associations, the relationship between Gaelic and Scottish national identity is both weak (with Scottish national identity and nationalist movements, past and present, placing relatively little emphasis on language issues) and contested (with some failing to accept Gaelic's national status and national relevance) (McLeod, 2001). The perceived connection between language and identity in Wales and the Basque Country inspires significant support for language development policies among politicians, policy-makers and ordinary voters, while in Scotland Gaelic is rarely prioritised and policy responses are characterised by a pervasive lack of urgency (Buchanan, 2002).

At another level, there is a significantly higher degree of what may be called language loyalty or ethno-linguistic vitality in the Welsh-speaking and Basque-speaking communities than in the Gaelic-speaking community in Scotland. Gaelic has had a minority status in Scotland for centuries, and has long been devalued by the Scottish mainstream and many of its own speakers, while Welsh and Basque, although also long marginalised by 'big' languages, have benefited from nationalist initiatives for more than a century and from recent development programmes that make bilingualism appear useful, valuable and relevant. The divergence in ethno-linguistic vitality may be seen most clearly in the differing levels of intergenerational language transmission. If two parents in the Basque Country speak Basque, they pass the language to their children effectively 100% of the time; in Wales, the rate is some 94%; but in Scotland, the rate is only 73% (and a mere 60% among Gaelic speakers in Lowland Scotland) (Azurmendi et al., 2001, p.246; MacKinnon, 1995). Even in Gaelic-speaking communities, then, there are difficulties in advancing strong Gaelic education programmes, a problem manifested most clearly in the low (some 26%) rate of uptake for GME in the Western Isles, an area in which some 61% of the population speaks Gaelic. In equivalent communities in Wales and the Basque Country, where doubts about the importance and value of the minority language have largely been dispelled, education through the minority language is effectively universal. The relationship between language, nationalism and identity in Ireland is unusually complex, as is the pattern of the development of Irish-medium education. As a result of the catastrophic decline of the Irish language in the nineteenth century, Irish nationalists made the restoration of the national language a key objective. Following independence for the southern twenty-six counties in 1922, Irish-medium education grew rapidly, but over time the state's commitment to Irish faded, and Irish-medium education began to wither. There were 284 Irish-medium primary schools in 1938 (outside the small areas designated as Irish-speaking), but only 22 in 1978 (Ó Murchú 2002, p.19). Since the early 1970s, however, a new, grass-roots movement for Irish-medium education has developed, and this has brought about a new wave of energy and innovation. Similarly, there has been rapid growth in the six counties of Northern Ireland since the 1970s: where Irish was once viewed with aggressive suspicion by the authorities, and confined to the margin of the curriculum in Catholic schools, Irish-medium schools have gone from strength to strength in recent years. The Irish language remains weak in comparison to Welsh and Basque, if still stronger than Gaelic in Scotland: more than 1.5 million people recorded themselves as Irish speakers in the last censuses (North and South), some 30% of the population of the island, but it is thought that at best a fifth of that number have a high active competence in the language, and only about 75,000 people use Irish on a daily basis (Mercator-Education, 2001 [Ó Murchú], p.5). There is a wide gap between rhetorical expressions of support for the language and genuine commitment to its use.

These differences in political and ethnolinguistic context are crucial, for the specific policy initiatives that have been put in place in the different countries are the consequence of the decisions and desires of both the minority language communities and the general population. That is to say, although minority language educational policy consists in a range of essentially technical structures and programmes, it is not possible simply to adopt what may in technical terms be best practice unless the political context is such as to make this outcome achievable. For example, despite an apparent consensus among education professionals and Gaelic education campaigners in Scotland that free-standing Gaelic schools offer significant advantages in comparison to Gaelic units appended to English-medium schools (the normal mode of GME delivery at present) (Johnstone, 1999), progress on this front has been slowed for essentially political reasons and evidence concerning minority-language development has played a minor role in decision-making. As such, although there are many potential lessons from the Welsh, Basque and

Irish experiences, it is doubtful to what extent these may be implemented given the less favourable political context in Scotland.

Welsh-medium education in Wales

Throughout the twentieth century Welsh-medium education has been more advanced than GME and has been considered more positively by the educational authorities. In no small measure, these successes have been achieved through sustained political campaigning and parental pressure. Today Welsh is institutionalised as part of the National Curriculum in Wales (by virtue of the Education Reform Act 1988) and all schools in Wales must offer Welsh to pupils until they reach the age of 16. The scale of Welsh-medium education in Wales is much greater than that of Gaelic-medium education in Scotland, as seen in Table 3. At the same time, analysts complain that the system has developed in an ad hoc, unintegrated fashion, 'without sight of clear or agreed destinations' (Baker & Prys Jones, 2000, p.136).

By 1917 (one year before Gaelic education was given its first, very modest statutory basis in Scotland) the Welsh Department had authorised the teaching of 'any of the subjects in the curriculum' through the medium of Welsh, and Welsh-medium teaching expanded steadily if slowly during the first half of the twentieth century (Evans, 2000). In 1939 the first bilingual Welsh school was set up by a group of concerned parents in Aberystwyth under the auspices of Urdd Gobaith Cymru (a cultural organisation comparable to An Comunn Gaidhealach in Scotland). Pursuant to a provision in the Education Act of 1944 that authorised local educational authorities to open Welsh-medium schools, the first Welsh primary school run by a local educational authority opened in Llanelli in 1947. By 1953 there were fourteen Welsh-medium primary schools in Wales attended by almost one thousand pupils; Welsh-medium secondary schools emerged from 1956 onwards, the first opening in Rhyl in Flintshire (Baker & Jones, 2000, p.117; Aitchison & Carter, 2000, pp.44–5). Significantly, Welsh-medium schools developed principally in urban areas where Welsh was not widely used at community level, rather than in the rural Welsh-speaking heartland (*Y Fro Gymraeg*), reflecting the commitment of parents to transmit and maintain Welsh in all parts of Wales.

In the early years Welsh-medium Education catered largely for children from Welsh-speaking homes but since the 1960s increasing numbers of learners have come into the system. Today, as with Gaelic in Scotland, Welsh-medium education caters for both pupils from Welsh-speaking homes and learners of Welsh (with the proportion of first-language speakers being higher in Welsh-speaking parts of Wales). Pupils of both kinds are usually taught together; the balancing between teaching for language maintenance (developing the skills of first-language speakers) and teaching for language acquisition (developing the skills of second-language learners) is no easy matter (Mercator-Education, 2001, [Jones], p.10; Gruffudd, 1999). Despite these difficulties, research suggests that Welsh-medium schools achieve educational outcomes superior to their English-medium counterparts, and give their pupils 'a competitive edge' (Reynolds et al., 1998) because of their supportive, holistic environment and because of the cognitive benefits of bilingualism.

In 1988 the Education Reform Act made Welsh a core subject in the National Curriculum in Welsh-medium schools and a foundation subject in other schools. In 1990 Welsh became a compulsory subject for all pupils in Wales at Key Stages 1, 2 and 3 (i.e. from ages 5 to 14) and in 1999 this requirement was extended to Key Stage 4 (i.e. up to age 16) (Mercator-Education, 2001, [Jones], p.9). This institutionalisation of Welsh education at a national level has been of immense significance.

Welsh-medium pre-school education began in 1949 and is now well-established throughout Wales, with Mudiad Ysgolion Meithrin, the Welsh Medium nursery association, playing a key role. Cylchoedd Meithrin (Welsh Medium nursery schools) and Cylchoedd Ti a Fi (literally 'You and I Circles') are in operation throughout Wales and are attended by some 13,000 children, the majority of them from non-Welsh-speaking homes (Aitchison & Carter 2000, pp.45, 140; Mercator-Education, 2001, [Jones], pp.14–15).

As with Gaelic in Scotland, local education authorities take different approaches to Welsh provision. In the traditionally Welsh-speaking areas (notably Gwynedd, where some 94% of primary schools are Welsh-medium), a general bilingual policy has been the norm: the goal is to ensure that all children can speak, read and write fluently and confidently in both Welsh and English by the time they move on to secondary school (Baker, 1993, pp.13–19; Baker and Prys Jones, 2000, pp.117–18). This policy is much more proactive than the approach taken by Comhairle nan Eilean (Siar), the authority for the Western Isles, which seeks to ensure only that Gaelic-speaking children become functionally bilingual and does not seek to ensure that *all* pupils leave primary school with equal competence in Gaelic and English (Comhairle nan Eilean Siar, 1996, p.9).

In areas of Wales where Welsh is less strong, designated Welsh schools have been established, at both primary and secondary level, and here Welsh is the normal teaching medium. Welsh is taught as a subject in the remaining schools. Although the teaching of Welsh as a subject has expanded dramatically in recent years as a result of the language's increased stature in the National Curriculum (described above), there has been little growth in the Welsh-medium sector in recent years, a trend some find troubling.

As with minority-language education in Scotland and many other countries, Welsh-medium education is less developed at secondary level than at primary level and the proportion of pupils receiving Welsh-medium education is lower. The system is continuing to grow, however, and local authorities are shedding their traditional reluctance to teach Mathematics and Science through the medium of Welsh, recognising that abstract concepts can be fully and adequately explained and communicated (Mercator-Education, 2001, [Jones], pp.20–1). One significant cause for concern, however, is that some 40% of children coming up from Welsh-medium Primary Education choose to move from the first-language to the second-language Welsh category in secondary school (Baker & Prys Jones, 2000, p.131).

Welsh-medium provision in the Further Education and Higher Education sectors is less developed. Until the 1980s FE provision was small-scale and generally confined to business, secretarial and care/nursery education. A development project from 1986-93 brought about an expansion, although this proved temporary; in recent years the Welsh Language Board has made growth in this sector a priority and it is expected that an increasing range of vocational and professional courses will come to be offered through Welsh, particularly as the role of Welsh in economic life continues to expand (Mercator-Education, 2001, [Jones], pp.24–5). At present only some 3% of FE students are assessed in Welsh (Baker & Prys Jones, 2000, pp.132–3). In the HE sector, teacher training for Welsh-medium education is available in seven of the eight teacher training institutions in Wales, with Welsh being the normal teaching medium for students entering the Welsh Medium sector. Prospective English Medium primary teachers have the option of studying Welsh as a component of their training course, so as to ensure that they can teach Welsh in English schools, in furtherance of the National Curriculum.

Welsh is relatively little used in teaching other subjects in the higher education sector, however. Since the 1950s there have been proposals to set up a Welsh-medium college within the University of Wales, but the authorities have preferred instead to make appointments within the existing colleges for the specific purpose of teaching subjects (other than Welsh language and literature) through the medium of Welsh. At present only some two dozen teaching staff in the University of Wales, out of approximately 5,000, fit into this category; most of these are in the University Colleges of Bangor and Aberystwyth. A University Board for Welsh-medium Teaching, which represents both the University of Wales and the post-1993 HE institutions in Wales, has now been established, but critics complain of tokenism and window-dressing (Mercator-Education, 2001, [Jones], pp.27–9; Wyn Jones et al., 2002).

In contrast, the demand for Welsh language courses in the Adult Education sector continues to grow: in 1999–2000 some 23,634 adults were enrolled in Welsh language courses of one kind or another, most of which are organised by HE or FE institutions or by Community Education departments. Eight Welsh for Adults consortia have responsibility for co-ordinating Welsh provision in the different parts of Wales (Mercator-Education, 2001, [Jones], pp.31–2). However, some critics comment that provision remains unintegrated and that the potential for adult learners in language revitalisation remains substantially untapped (Morris, 2000).

A key problem in contemporary Wales involves the gap between language acquisition and language use. By virtue of the systematic development described above, the education system has succeeded in producing large numbers of young people who leave school as Welsh-English bilinguals, but in most cases they live in English-dominant environments, and it is questionable to what extent they actually use Welsh in their daily interactions and will continue to do so over the course of their lives. As Joshua Fishman has explained, this is a crucial difficulty arising from the use of the education system as an instrument of linguistic revitalisation (Fishman, 1991, pp.398–402). Thus, the facts that overall numbers of Welsh speakers are rising, especially in urban parts of Wales, and that increasing proportions of young people have the ability to speak Welsh, by no means guarantee the security of Welsh for the future; the proportion of children who use Welsh as their first language in the home continues to decline (Gruffudd, 1999; Gruffudd, 2000). Gaelic in Scotland remains in a much poorer state, with overall speaker numbers still dropping and the number of pupils entering GME each year still less than one-fifth of the number of Gaelic speakers who die each year. Nevertheless, the Welsh (and Basque) experience demonstrates that even if GME were to expand five- or six-fold, and the overall number of persons able to speak Gaelic stabilised, critical problems would remain. Fishman has correctly warned that language revitalisation strategies that place excessive emphasis on the education system are most unlikely to succeed, and his trenchant warning that Gaelic initiatives in Scotland have placed 'well nigh complete reliance on the school and other higher order "props"' remains fundamentally valid (Fishman, 1991, p.380).

Basque-medium education in the Basque Country

The rapid growth of Basque-medium education has been even more impressive than the development of Welsh, an achievement that is all the more remarkable given the severe repression of the language during the years of the Franco dictatorship (1937–75), when the public use of Basque was illegal. As with Gaelic in Scotland, numbers of Basque speakers dropped precipitously during the first three quarters of the twentieth century, but since the enactment of the Statute of Autonomy in 1979 and the Basic Law on the Standardisation of Basque in 1982, a comprehensive programme of 'Basquisation' has brought about a significant growth in the number of Basque speakers (from 21.6% of the population in 1981 to 30.9% in 1996) and strengthened the language in all aspects of Basque life. The expansion of Basque in the education system has played a key role.

Four different models of education exist (or have existed) in the Basque Country in recent years, known as Models D, B, A and X, (there is no letter 'C' in Basque.) In Model D, a total immersion model, almost all teaching is carried out through the medium of Basque, with Spanish being taught as a subject. Following years of steady progress, and ever-increasing parental demand, this model has now become dominant. In Model B, an early partial immersion programme, teaching is carried out roughly half in Basque and half in Spanish (although in practice there is much diversity from area to area and school to school). In Model A, almost all teaching is carried out in Spanish, with Basque being taught as a subject. In Model X — once the only model but now almost nonexistent — only Spanish is used and Basque is not taught (Gardner, 2002, § 4.4.2.1; Lasagabaster, 2001, pp.410–12). Table 4 indicates the current situation with regard to Models B and D. The growth of Model D since the early 1980s has been remarkable, as shown in Table 5.

Basque-medium education initiatives began in the early decades of the twentieth century but these were stopped and indeed banned by the Franco regime. In the early 1960s, politically committed parents began to establish clandestine Basque-medium schools known as *ikastolak*. Slowly these *ikastolak* began to receive a modicum of toleration from the authorities and by the time of Franco's death in 1975 some 10% of primary pupils were enrolled in this sector. Growth then became rapid with the coming of liberalisation and then autonomy after 1978. In 1993 the government required the *ikastolak* either to join the state sector or forego the special funding arrangements they had previously received; some 35% joined the state sector, but some 65%, typically the larger and better-established schools, chose to remain private (Mercator-Education 2000, [Gardner], p.5; Lasagabaster, 2001, p.408). In accordance with Fishman's typology, which differentiates between schools controlled by the minority-language community and schools controlled by state authorities, the private *ikastolak* tend to maintain a more intensely Basque environment (Fishman, 1991, pp.98–103; Gardner, 2002, § 5.2.3).

Most schools, including the *ikastolak*, contain streams of different models. Typically first-language Basque-speaking children (almost all of whom study under Model D) are taught together with learners undergoing Basque immersion, as in Scotland and Wales, but in some schools the two groups are kept separate (Lasagabaster, 2001, pp.410–11). Basque-medium teaching is naturally more prevalent in parts of the country where Basque is more widely spoken. The private educational sector is much larger in the Basque Country than in Scotland, enrolling about half of all pupils (although, as in Scotland, the majority of these schools are Catholic institutions funded by the state); here Basque-medium teaching is not as common, except in those *ikastolak* that elected to remain outside the state sector after 1993 (Mercator-Education, 2000, [Gardner], p.4; Lasagabaster, 2001, p.408).

As with Gaelic in Scotland and Welsh in Wales, Basque-medium education becomes less prevalent as one moves upwards in the system, reaching over 60% of pupils in infant education and 50% in primary education, but only 35% in secondary education (compulsory and post-compulsory). Some pupils move from Model B to Model A at secondary level; a matter for concern in Wales as well, as noted above. Basque-medium teaching is much weaker in secondary technical/vocational education (some 13% following Model D) than in the academic (university preparatory) stream (some 40%); this disparity may have negative ramifications for the use of Basque in employment. Numbers are lower still in the university sector, but the scale is much greater than anything known in Wales, let alone Scotland. At the University of the Basque Country (one of three universities in the Basque Country but much the largest), some 55% of courses are offered through Basque but only 20% of students receive even part of their teaching in Basque (Mercator-Education, 2000, [Gardner], pp.13–14; Etxeberria, 2001). Formal plans for the tertiary sector anticipate that by 2005, 50% of students will complete their degrees in Basque, but there is doubt as to whether this target will be achieved, even though targeted hiring since 1990 has brought about a significant increase (to approximately 25%) in the proportion of teaching staff who can teach through Basque (Gardner, 2000, § 6.3; Lasagabaster, 2001, p.419).

A critical problem facing educationalists in the Basque Country has been the steady decline in school rolls due to a major drop in the birth rate (almost 60% between 1976 and 1997). This has meant that the demand for teachers has decreased significantly and that there have been very few entrants to the teaching profession in recent years. This downturn has, in turn, presented significant challenges for the 'Basquisation' process: in-service rather than initial training has been the principal mechanism for producing the teaching staff necessary to meet the increased demand for Basque-medium education.

The Basque education authorities have risen to this challenge and developed a comprehensive and highly successful programme for retraining teachers for Basque-medium education, beginning in 1981–82. Teachers in the public sector who enrol on these Basque courses are entitled to up to three years' full-time release on full pay, with the state also paying the cost of a replacement teacher. (Payments for the retraining of private sector teachers are slightly less generous). In each recent school year, well over a thousand teachers have been enrolled on such courses; the annual budget for the programme is now approximately 1.4 million euro. In 1976–77 only some 5% of public school teachers knew Basque, but by 1998 some 56% of primary and secondary teachers had gained certificates for Basque-medium teaching (Mercator-Education, 2000, [Gardner], pp.15–16). Counterpart efforts in Scotland have been on a very small scale and with minimal funding, and the chronic problem of teacher shortage has very largely been considered in terms of initial rather than in-service training. However, Scotland has only recently begun to face the problem of taking on teaching candidates who may not have reached native-level competence in the language, a problem which has long been present in the Basque Country and elsewhere, notably Ireland (Gardner, 2001).

Another remarkable success in the Basque Country has been the development of adult education in Basque since the 1970s. Together with some private learning organisations, the Institute for Basquisation and Literacy for Adult plays a key role in co-ordinating provision, developing teaching materials, training specialist teachers, and monitoring and evaluating the teaching and learning of Basque. There are now some 150 government-run and private *euskaltegiak* or Basque language schools, which offer intensive training in the language for those seeking to gain fluency and literacy courses for adult fluent speakers. Some 50,000 students attend Basque language courses each year, a plurality of them in the 21–30 age group (Mercator-Education, 2000, [Gardner], pp.16–18; Azurmendi et al., 2001, pp.244–5). Through these efforts literacy in Basque has been dramatically increased and fluent adult learners of Basque have become commonplace; in contrast, Gaelic literacy rates remain low. Approximately 63% of Gaelic speakers could read Gaelic and approximately 47% could write it. Literacy rates for English amongst Gaelic speakers are probably over 95%. Gaelic learners remain both scarce and marginal (MacCaluim, 2002).

Language planners in the Basque Country place great emphasis on connecting Basque-medium education to language use in family, social and economic life. Sociolinguistic research suggests that the actual use of Basque has increased in recent years, not simply the capacity to use it. A 'virtuous circle' of sorts has developed: as more parents choose Model D education with the view that it will secure their children's command of Basque and increase their life opportunities, the demand for Basque-medium services and the ability to deliver them increase in turn. Nevertheless, although there are many positive signs of increased Basque use, the sustainability of these gains is open to question, and Spanish retains its overwhelming dominance. There are major challenges in linguistic, sociolinguistic and political terms, from concerns about the kind of Basque, heavily influenced by Spanish, that is spoken by many school-taught learners to the complex relationship between language policy, Basque nationalism and Spanish nationalism (Azurmendi et al., 2001; Gardner, 2002).

Irish-medium education in Ireland

The course of development of Irish-medium education has been more tortuous than the history of Welsh or Basque education. The institutional-isation of Irish in the education system began early in the twentieth century, but then underwent a decline, only to be followed by a new wave of activity and energy that continues today, on both sides of the border.

The Irish language declined extraordinarily rapidly during the nineteenth century: where almost half the population spoke Irish in 1800, by 1926 only some 3% lived in Irish-speaking districts, which were very largely confined to the poorest and remotest parts of the country (Ó Riagáin, 1997, p.4, p.271). From the 1880s onwards nationalist activists made the restoration of Irish a central objective. Sustained political pressure led to the introduction of Irish as a subject in national schools in 1900 and as a teaching medium in 1904, and to the establishment of the first Irish-medium (private) school in 1908; by 1915–16 Irish was the teaching medium in roughly half the primary schools in the Irish-speaking districts and by 1921 a quarter of primary school children in Ireland were studying Irish (Ó Huallacháin, 1994, pp.54–6, pp.119–20; Hindley, 1991, pp.23–4).

When the southern twenty-six counties of Ireland gained independence from Britain in 1922, the teaching of Irish, particularly in primary schools, was viewed as the key instrument of a national language revival (Ó Riagáin, 1997, pp.15–17). There was a great sense of optimism, optimism that appears immensely naive in hindsight, as when Timothy Corcoran argued in 1925 that 'the popular schools can give and restore our native language, they can do it without positive aid from the home' (quoted in Ó Laoire, 2002, p.83). Irish became a centrepiece of the national curriculum, so that all schoolchildren studied the language and Irish became the normal medium for infant education; Irish-medium education became universal in the designated Irish-speaking areas (known as the *Gaeltacht*) and also grew rapidly in the English-speaking parts of the Free State, so that by 1940–41 some 12.3% of primary schools were teaching entirely through Irish and a further 43.2% of schools were teaching partly through Irish (Ó Riagáin, 1997, p.16; Ó Huallacháin, 1994, pp.120–41).

Yet neither the purported national language restoration nor the teaching of Irish in the schools achieved the desired results, in part because for many the commitment to Irish was more rhetorical than real (MacPóilin, 1997). A period of retrenchment began in the late 1950s, driven in part by a public backlash against the perceived deficiencies of Irish-medium education (Hindley, 1991, pp.37–8; MacNamara, 1966). In sum, the basic state objective shifted from a policy of wholesale language restoration to one of language maintenance and the mere servicing of the existing Irish-speaking population, as demonstrated most obviously by the decisions in 1973 to abandon the Irish requirement for school leavers and entrants to the civil service (Ó Riagáin, 1997, p.22, pp.270–71; Ó Riagain, 2001; Ó Murchú, 2002). As part of this retrenchment, the number of Irish-medium primary schools had declined to 43 by 1970 and a mere 22 by 1978, and efforts to use Irish as a teaching medium were largely replaced by emphasis on teaching Irish as a subject (Ó Murchú, 2002, p.19; Ó Riagáin, 1997, p.21).

From the early 1970s onwards, however, a new, bottom-up movement for Irish-medium education began to take root. Concern among parents committed to the Irish language but dissatisfied with the failures of state-directed language policy in education led to the establishment of a new organisation, Gaelscoileanna (initially known as Coiste Náisiúnta na Scoileanna Lán-Ghaeilge) in 1973, with the aim of setting up independent, all-Irish schools. Many such schools began in temporary premises, with a small group of dedicated parents coming together to pay a teacher (Mercator-Education, 2001, [Ó Murchú], p.12). The parent-driven all-Irish schools have gone from strength to strength, driven by strong demand commensurate with their excellent educational results, and have become a major source of energy and enthusiasm in the Irish language movement in the Republic (Ní Fhearghusa, 2002, pp.43–5). In school year 2002–03 there are 119 Irish-medium primary schools in the Republic (not including those in the *Gaeltacht*, whose distinct situation is discussed below), spread out through 25 of the 26 counties, with a total of 21,894 pupils in 2002–03, some 5.5% of the total number outwith the *Gaeltacht*. The great majority of children come from English-speaking backgrounds, although some parents (more commonly second-language learners than native speakers) do use Irish at home to some extent. There has been a strong preference for dedicated schools, with their solidly Irish-language environment, instead of units within larger English-medium schools (which has been the prevalent structure in Scotland) (Ní Fhearghusa, 2000, pp.30–31; Ní Fhearghusa, 2002).

Despite the scale of institutional development and the state's purported commitment to Irish, significant problems remain with regard to the provision of teaching materials and other educational resources (Ní Fhearghusa, 2002, pp.45–6). Accommodation is still often much less than ideal, with many schools housed in substandard or temporary quarters; start-up state funding is only provided when 17 pupils (not previously attending any other school) are enrolled, and 95% funding of operating costs is only provided when 55 pupils are enrolled, so that parents must undertake considerable fund-raising efforts in the initial stages (Ní Fhearghusa, 2002).

Irish-medium provision at secondary level is much less developed, and, as in Scotland, this lack of continuity has become a major source of concern in recent years. In the school year 2002–03 there were 31 Irish-medium secondary schools in the Republic (outside the *Gaeltacht*), located in 14 of the 26 counties, with a total of 5,223 pupils in attendance in 2002–03, some 1.7% of the total number of secondary pupils outwith the *Gaeltacht*. The Department of Education requires minimum numbers of pupils before it will authorise an Irish-medium secondary school, a threshold that can be difficult to reach; in a number of cases, especially outside large urban areas, Irish-medium units have been established within English-medium schools, but these have often been unsuccessful, leading to dissatisfaction among parents and pupils, and an unwillingness to opt for Irish-medium education at secondary level (Ní Fhearghusa, 2000, pp.30–31; Ní Fhearghusa, 2002, pp.46–7).

Irish (as as subject, generally taught through Irish) remains part of the core curriculum during the years of compulsory schooling (6–15) and roughly three-quarters of all secondary pupils take Irish to Leaving Certificate level (comparable to the Higher in Scotland), not least because the constituent colleges of National University of Ireland (four of the Republic's seven universities) and the teacher training colleges continue to require applicants to take the Leaving Certificate examination in Irish. However, the proportion of students who do not take Irish to Leaving Certificate level, or who fail the examination, has been increasing steadily in recent years, while overall levels of attainment in Irish have been declining (Ó Riagáin, 1997, pp.213–15).

Since the early twentieth century, there has been a network of Irish-medium preschools (*naíonraí*) in place. In 2002–2003, there were 210 *naíonraí* in the Republic (69 in *Gaeltacht* areas and 141 in the rest of the Republic), serving some 3,200 children. Approximately two-thirds of the children in attendance arrive with little or no Irish (Mercator-Education, 2001, [Ó Murchú], p.16).

Compared to provision for Irish in schools in the English-speaking parts of the Republic, there has been more continuity in Gaeltacht schools, where Irish has been the teaching medium since the establishment of the Free State. In 2000–2001, there were 105 Irish-medium primary schools in the *Gaeltacht*, serving 7,181 pupils and 20 post-primary schools, serving 3,329 pupils. Crucially, however, today's *Gaeltacht* is by no means a monolingual Irish-speaking area: only 74% of the *Gaeltacht* population of approximately 86,000 can speak Irish (a number that includes many second-language speakers as well as native speakers) and only about 36.5% of *Gaeltacht* residents actually use the language on a daily basis (although the proportion in the strongest Irish-speaking areas exceeds 85%) (Coimisiún na Gaeltachta, 2002, pp.9–10, pp.21–4). This figure also excludes the 5–19 age group, where the rate of daily usage is likely to be around 58.4% as a result of Irish-medium education. (Coimisiun na Gaeltachta, 2002, p.23). A combination of language shift, return migration and in-migration means that Irish-medium schools in the *Gaeltacht* are becoming increasingly bilingual, serving both native Irish-speaking children and native English-speaking children with varying levels of competence in Irish (Mercator-Education 2001, [Ó Murchú], p.11; Ó Murchadha, 2001, pp.88–94). As in Wales, the Basque Country, and indeed Scotland, teaching such a mixed group gives rise to significant pedagogical challenges.

Irish has only a limited role in further and higher education, although it has long been the normal teaching medium in the various Irish departments. A BA course in Business and Communication is available at Galway-Mayo Institute of Technology and a Diploma in Office Information Systems is available at Letterkenny Institute of Technology (see Comhar na Múinteoirí Gaeilge, 2003, pp.34–5). Because of its proximity to the largest and strongest of the Irish-speaking districts, University College Galway (now National University of Ireland, Galway) was in 1929 given a special responsibility to teach subjects through the medium of Irish, but the extent of Irish-medium provision (outside the Faculty of Celtic Studies) has diminished over time; courses in Commerce, French, Geography, History and Physical Sciences are currently available, but enrolments are low (see Comhar na Múinteoirí Gaeilge, 2003, pp.13–19). More recently, several degree courses taught through Irish have been developed at FIONTAR in the Business School of Dublin City University (see Comhar na Múinteoirí Gaeilge, 2003, pp.25–7), and Irish-medium postgraduate courses at the University of Limerick (in Applied Sociolinguistics) and NUI Galway (in Translation studies, Information Technology and Applied Communications) will be delivered from 2003–04. Discussions are ongoing about ways of developing Irish-medium higher education, including a potential all-Irish institution, but there is as yet no clear commitment from the authorities (Walsh, forthcoming).

Each of the five teacher training colleges in the Republic teaches partly through the medium of Irish, as all primary teachers must be capable of teaching through Irish; one of the smaller colleges, Coláiste Mhuire, Marino, conducts almost all its teaching through Irish. There have long been concerns about the level of teaching candidates' attainment in Irish, however, and the ramifications for pupils of this underperformance. There are no courses specifically designed to train Irish-medium teachers in the Republic; in addition, such a course has now been established in the North, as discussed below (Mercator-Education, 2001, [Ó Murchú], pp.31–3).

The position of Irish in the six counties of Northern Ireland after partition in 1920 was profoundly different from that of the Free State/Republic. Irish had nearly died out as a traditional community language by 1920, so there was and is no real question of language maintenance, only of revival. The Unionist authorities were bitterly hostile to Irish, and Irish was essentially confined to Catholic schools, but provision for the language in this sector was nowhere near as extensive as in the Free State/Republic (Maguire, 1991; Mac Póilin, 1997, 2000). In 1950, for example, only 7.3% of primary school children were studying Irish; in 1969–70, only some 6% (or some 12% of Catholic pupils) studied Irish (Hindley, 1991, pp.152–3).

From the early 1970s onwards, however, a deeply committed Irish-language movement has developed in Northern Ireland, and the growth of Irish-medium education has been rapid. The first initiatives in Irish-medium education, beginning in West Belfast in 1971, were denied state support; indeed the parents who founded the first Irish-medium school, Bunscoil Phobal Feirste, were threatened with prosecution (Maguire, 1991, pp.67–78). Only in 1983 did the state begin to fund Irish-medium education, beginning with an Irish-medium unit in a Derry primary school, with Bunscoil Phobal Feirste receiving state support from 1984 onwards (Peover, 2001, pp.200–01; Mercator-Education,1997, [Mac Póilin], p.10). The dynamic of political oppositionalism, indeed outright resistance to the state, that has driven much Irish-language campaigning in Northern Ireland (including campaigns for Irish-medium education) is quite unknown in Scotland (Mac Póilin, 1997, pp.186–7). So too is the intensity of the suspicion and hostility that sections of the Unionist population have expressed towards Irish-language initiatives of any kind (Mac Póilin, 2000).

In the school year 2002–03 there were 25 Irish-medium primary schools (located in five of the six counties), with a total of 1,996 pupils in attendance (approximately 1.2% of the total). This number is slightly higher than the figure for Gaelic-medium in Scotland, although Scotland has more than three times the population of Northern Ireland. 19 of these schools are now receiving state funding; where the viability criteria for funding of Irish-medium primary schools once presented significant obstacles, thresholds have recently been lowered, so that state funding will now be given to schools in Belfast and Derry having at least 15 pupils (the main urban areas) and 12 pupils elsewhere (Peover, 2001, pp. 199–203). In contrast to Scotland, there has been a strong preference in Northern Ireland for dedicated all-Irish schools, although there are some Irish-medium units within larger English-medium primary schools.

Secondary education through Irish has also grown in Northern Ireland, although as with minority-language educational initiatives in other countries, it lags behind primary education. The first Irish-medium secondary school was established in west Belfast in 1991 and received state funding from 1996 onwards; two Irish-medium units in secondary schools, one in Derry and one in Armagh, have been established more recently. There were a total of 417 pupils enrolled in these secondary schools/units in 2002–03 (approximately 0.03% of the total).

In recent years, and especially since the Good Friday Agreement of 1997, Irish-medium education in Northern Ireland has received greatly increased state support and has become 'normalised' in many respects (cf. McCoy, 2001). The Department of Education now has a statutory obligation 'to encourage and facilitate the development of Irish-medium education', and a range of institutional structures have been put in place, including a new support organisation, Comhairle na Gaelscolaíochta (the Council for Irish-medium Education) Iontaobhas na Gaelscolaíochta a new trust that seeks to provide support for Irish-medium schools that have not yet gained official recognition and funding. Dedicated training courses (BEd and PGCE) for Irish-medium primary teachers have been established at St Mary's College, Belfast, to underpin the development of the Irish-medium sector (Peover, 2002; Nig Uidhir, 2002).

Despite these various initiatives, the future of the Irish language remains uncertain: there is now more talk of survival than of revival (Ó Riagáin, 2001, p.209). Yet it is important to emphasise the policy successes, limited as these are, as well as the failures. Although the traditional Irish-speaking community in the *Gaeltacht*, in which the language has been transmitted without interruption from generation to generation, has become increasingly frail, its position would without question be far worse in the absence of eighty years' proactive state support, including near-universal Irish-medium education in these districts (Ó Riagáin, 1997, pp.141–2). Similarly, the institutionalisation of Irish in the education system (both as a teaching medium and as a subject) has meant that in successive generations substantial numbers of people from non-Irish-speaking homes (concentrated in the upper socio-economic groups) have successfully acquired Irish, even if a clear majority of those taught Irish do not gain active competence in the language (Ó Riagain, 1997, pp.193–4; Ó Riagain, 2001, pp.204–06). There are obvious limits to this strategy: each generation must start afresh, so to speak, for there is no meaningful process of self-sustaining language transmission (Mac Póilin, 1997, pp.178–80). Given the decline of the *Gaeltacht* and the limits of school-based transmission, the position of Irish is certainly much less secure than that of Welsh or Basque, and the fact that the great majority of Irish speakers are second-language learners creates a range of difficulties (Ó Baoill, 1999; Maguire, 1991, pp.186–228).

Conclusion

In educational and linguistic terms, Gaelic, Welsh, Basque and Irish face very similar problems: how to develop teaching methods and materials to introduce a once-excluded language into the curriculum, how to immerse children in a new language, how to turn school learners of a language into confident users of that language, how to connect school-based learning to broader linguistic revitalisation efforts, and so on. As such, the Welsh, Basque and Irish examples can provide extremely valuable lessons for Scotland. At the same time, Welsh, Basque and Irish education are carried out on a much greater scale than Gaelic education, and are more firmly embedded in educational structures and institutions. Only a few decades ago, however, both Welsh and Basque education were as frail as Gaelic education is today, and faced difficulties that were at least as challenging. Similarly, the recent growth of Irish education in Northern Ireland has outpaced the development of Gaelic, despite having had to confront significantly greater obstacles. Whether Gaelic in Scotland can successfully emulate these examples depends in large measure on the political commitment of Scottish decision-makers and, indeed, the Gaelic community itself.

Table 3: Comparative figures from Welsh/Gaelic medium provision

	Wales	Scotland
Total number of children attending Welsh/ Gaelic-medium preschool units playgroups	13359	2423
Total number of Welsh/Gaelic-medium preschool units/playgroups	1028	165
Total number of primary pupils	282558	420523
Number of primary pupils taught through Welsh/Gaelic	51344	1859
Primary pupils taught through the medium of Welsh/Gaelic as proportion of total (Note that of the primary pupils not receiving Welsh-medium teaching, more than 97% were being taught Welsh as a second language)	18.2	0.5%
Total number of primary schools	1624	2278
Number of primary schools teaching wholly or predominantly through Welsh/Gaelic (This figure takes in all the secondary schools that teach some subjects through the medium of Gaelic. In addition to the 52 designated Welsh secondary schools, a further 9 secondary schools in Wales teach some subjects through the medium of Welsh)	440	59
Primary schools teaching through the medium of Welsh/Gaelic as proportion of total	27.1%	2.6%
Total number of secondary pupils	187112	316400
Secondary pupils taught Welsh/Gaelic as first language	26967	928
Secondary pupils taught Welsh/Gaelic as a first language as proportion of total	14.4%	0.3%
Secondary pupils taught Welsh/Gaelic as a second language	158185	2131
Secondary pupils taught Welsh/Gaelic as a second language as proportion of total	84.5%	0.7%
Total number of secondary schools	227	387
Number of Welsh-/Gaelic-medium or bilingual secondary schools (This figure for Gaelic takes in all secondary schools teaching some subjects through the medium of Gaelic. A further 9 secondary schools in	52	14

Wales teacimg some subjects through the
medium of Welsh would be counted under
the Scottish enumeration method.)

Welsh-/Gaelic-medium or bilingual secondary schools as proportion of total	22.9%	3.6%

Numbers for Wales are for 2001–02 and are derived from the Welsh Schools' Census 2002 (compiled by the National Statistics Office) and from Welsh Language Board data.

Numbers of children enrolled in Gaelic-medium education in Scotland are for 2002–03 as compiled by the Faculty of Education, University of Strathclyde. Total numbers of pupils in Scotland are based on the Scottish Executive's 2001–02 Schools Census.

Table 4: Basque-medium education in the Basque Country

Total number of preschool pupils	60841
Number of preschool pupils taught through Basque (Model D)	37026
Number of preschool pupils taught through both Basque and Spanish (Model B)	17514
Preschool pupils taught through Basque (Model D) as proportion of total	60.9%
Total number of primary pupils	97156
Number of primary pupils taught through Basque (Model D)	48679
Number of primary pupils taught through both Basque and Spanish (Model B)	28305
Primary pupils taught through Basque (Model D) as proportion of total	50.1%
Total number of secondary pupils	146037
Number of primary pupils taught through Basque (Model D)	50834
Primary pupils taught through both Basque and Spanish (Model B)	21241
Secondary pupils taught through Basque (Model D) as proportion of total	34.8%

Note: Figures are for 2001–02 and are derived from EUSTAT (Basque Statistical Office) data.

Gaelic Medium Education

Table 5: Changes in the proportion of pupils aged 3–14 enrolled in different teaching models

	1983–4	1986–7	1990–1	1996–7	1998–9
Model A	72.9	64.1	50.7	31.5	26.0
Model B	10.5	15.9	24.9	27.8	28.0
Model D	16.6	20.0	24.5	40.7	45.0

Figures are derived from Lasagabaster, 2000, p.411.

CHAPTER 3

MANAGING PROVISION:
THE SCHOOL PERSPECTIVE

Rosemary Ward

Introduction

This chapter explores the issues surrounding the management of Gaelic Medium provision in schools. It examines the practical and methodological challenges facing managers and teaching staff involved in the delivery of GME. It seeks to demonstrate that a national strategy is essential to address current needs in Gaelic education. It contends that without effective national planning the future of Gaelic education will be significantly compromised. Finally, the chapter will touch on the role of parents and the wider community in enhancing school-based Gaelic learning.

A number of practical issues can affect the running of Gaelic-medium provision, and headteachers find themselves having to consider these when faced with the challenge of managing Gaelic-medium units in their schools. Interestingly, many of the general issues raised in this section apply equally to pre-school, primary and secondary establishments.

Prior to the establishment of Sgoil Ghàidhlig Ghlaschu (The Glasgow Gaelic School) in 1998, all Gaelic-medium provision took the form of Gaelic Medium Units (GMU) housed within mainstream education establishments. In recent times, most local authorities favour the use of words such as 'classes' or 'provision' rather than 'unit' to describe their Gaelic-medium delivery. The word 'unit' has connotations of difference and of being set apart and goes against a spirit of inclusion and integration. GME should not be seen as the 'cuckoo in the mainstream nest'. True inclusiveness depends on the realisation that the educational attainment and achievement of every individual needs to be fully developed, valued and respected. Managers of Gaelic-medium provision must strive to ensure that a range of opportunities exist to ensure that integration is brought about.

However, with the exception of Bunsgoil Ghàidhlig Ghlaschu, all other Gaelic-medium provision in Scotland is lodged within English mainstream schools. The choice of schools to host Gaelic-medium provision has never been based on an agreed set of educational criteria. Selection has usually been on the basis of availability of suitable classroom accommodation. As a result, Gaelic-medium provision is located in schools where there is vacant accommodation and not necessarily because the headteacher is knowledgeable or sympathetic towards bilingual education. It is against this background that we now consider the practical challenges.

The Language Barrier

The ability to speak Gaelic is not a pre-requisite for a headteacher of an establishment offering Gaelic-medium provision. While one would expect that many of the headteachers of Gaelic-medium establishments in the Western Isles and parts of the Highland Council area will indeed be Gaelic speakers, this is not the case in most of the other schools across Scotland. Many headteachers feel that not being able to speak Gaelic is a barrier to their ability to become actively involved in classroom practice in their Gaelic-medium classes. This is particularly true in the case of Gaelic immersion classes where the emphasis is on maintaining Gaelic usage at all times. Non-Gaelic-speaking headteachers do make an effort to learn a variety of simple words and phrases in order to welcome and praise Gaelic pupils where appropriate but it is impossible for them to engage in meaningful dialogue with Gaelic-medium pupils.

One example of best practice, observed in a school where the headteacher was not a Gaelic speaker, involved the headteacher visiting the Gaelic classes every other day, taking notice of new work displayed on walls or reviewing the work in pupils' books. She made a point of praising the pupils' efforts at every opportunity and drawing their attention to the work they had displayed on their classroom walls. Although the headteacher's medium for doing so was English, the pupils and teachers felt that their efforts were valued and that, although she could not speak Gaelic, she was nonetheless able to appreciate that good learning was taking place.

Supporting the needs of Gaelic-medium staff can be a problem for headteachers who are not Gaelic speakers themselves. Monitoring and evaluation of classroom practice can be difficult if the headteacher observing a class lesson does not understand the content of the lesson. There is no doubt that a good professional can tell whether or not meaningful learning and teaching is taking place irrespective of whether s/he can understand the medium for delivery. However, in order to be able to make a value judgement on the quality of education being delivered in

Gaelic-medium classes, many headteachers require the support of their local authority Quality Improvement Officers. This in itself is not without difficulty when one considers that of the fourteen Scottish local authorities currently making Gaelic-medium provision only three authorities employ Gaelic Quality Improvement Officers. Supporting the needs of Gaelic-medium teachers is less of a problem in large schools where there are a number of Gaelic-medium teachers. In these schools Gaelic-medium staff can support each others' development needs. It is not uncommon for a senior member of the Gaelic staff to assume responsibility for the improvement agenda for the Gaelic-medium classes. In such instances the headteacher would seek reassurances from this individual that needs were being met.

Unfortunately, very few support networks exist either for the Gaelic-medium teacher in the rural school with a composite class which may include pupils from primary 1–7, or for the Gaelic-medium teacher in a large primary school in a Scottish town. While headteachers can make every effort to ensure that these Gaelic teachers are supported and their efforts are recognised, it is very difficult for them to break down the feeling of isolation that many may experience in these circumstances. In some schools the Gaelic-medium teacher is the only Gaelic speaker whom the pupils will meet during their school day. These teachers do not have the luxury of being able to seek reassurances from fellow Gaelic teachers about their practice. The medium for communication in their staff-rooms is likely to be English and they may have very few opportunities to use their Gaelic with another adult outwith the classroom setting.

More has to be done to support the needs of the non-Gaelic-speaking headteachers who have management responsibility for Gaelic-medium provision across Scotland. One suggestion might entail the establishment of a forum for all such headteachers where they can share concerns and identify support mechanisms for each other. Annual meetings would allow for discussion of national and local developments and their implications for Gaelic-medium provision.

With regard to the issue of the sole Gaelic teacher employed in a small rural school or the developing central belt provision, the potential of ICT as a networking tool for isolated Gaelic-medium teachers must be investigated thoroughly. Efforts have to be made to ensure that these teachers feel they are supported and can access support from similarly placed colleagues. The alternative is that these teachers will become disaffected and seek employment outwith the Gaelic-medium context. Those are losses that GME can ill afford and which must be avoided at all costs.

Management Time
Management responsibility for Gaelic-medium provision rests with the respective headteachers of host establishments. Many headteachers feel that the establishment of Gaelic-medium provision in their schools presents them with a range of new and very distinct management challenges. Some might argue that they are taking on the management of two schools within one establishment.

Headteachers in these schools feel they should be given support to undertake the additional responsibilities associated with budget monitoring, administration, resource management and staffing of Gaelic-medium provision within their schools. This is a particular issue for class-committed headteachers of small rural establishments with Gaelic-medium classes. Not only do they have to teach the 5–14 curriculum and deal with management issues in their English-medium classes, they also have to monitor the effectiveness of the teaching within the Gaelic classes and take on the different management challenges that Gaelic education presents.

It is also the case that where Gaelic pre-school provision is available to match the primary provision, it is usually, although not always, located within the host establishment. The management responsibility for this also then rests with the headteacher. Even if Gaelic pre-school provision is located outwith the primary establishment, the headteacher will have been involved in the preparation of transition arrangements to ensure the smooth transfer of Gaelic pre-school children into Gaelic-medium immersion classes.

It is easy to see why time is often cited as a particular challenge for headteachers of Gaelic-medium provision. The many and varied demands placed on headteachers in a climate of constant educational change is often more acutely felt in establishments with Gaelic provision. It is important that all local authorities afford headteachers of Gaelic-medium provision enhanced management time to undertake their additional duties. It is also imperative that all local authorities provide appropriate induction training for headteachers faced with the challenge of managing new Gaelic-medium provision.

Teacher Supply and Recruitment
The acute national shortage of Gaelic-medium teachers is putting the development of new Gaelic provision in jeopardy. There are currently 150 Gaelic-medium primary teachers employed in full-time posts in 60 Gaelic-medium units across Scotland. A further 54 teachers are involved in the delivery of Gaelic and of other subjects through the medium of Gaelic in 34 secondary schools. In session 2001–02, local authorities involved in the delivery of GME projected that a total of 20 Gaelic-

medium teachers were required to fill actual vacancies. Given that there were only 15 graduates of GME in the Teacher Education Institutes (TEIs) in session 2001–02 it was inevitable that many Gaelic posts would remain vacant.

The shortage of Gaelic-medium teachers is not a new phenomenon. As early as 1995 the need for specific pre-service training for students wishing to teach in a Gaelic-medium setting was highlighted by Stradling and MacNeil. (1995). Newly qualified teachers reported that the pre-service course they had followed had not given them a clear insight into the demands of Gaelic-medium teaching. Nor had it been delivered by specialists with direct experience of Gaelic-medium teaching. Finally, there was no support for those students who were required to work on their own literacy skills development in GME.

In 1999, the GTCS published a report which called for a dedicated initial teacher education course delivered through the medium of Gaelic. This course would guarantee Gaelic-speaking students access to Gaelic-medium teaching placements and would specifically meets the linguistic development needs of pre-service students. This report was enthusiastically received by all involved in Gaelic education and by the many Gaelic agencies supporting Gaelic developments. To date, rather disappointingly, the Scottish Executive has failed to act on the recommendations in the GTCS report. In spite of expensive national advertising campaigns it remains difficult to attract sufficient numbers into Gaelic-medium teaching careers to meet the growing demand. This national teacher shortage has been felt most acutely in Highland rural areas and the islands of Argyll and Bute. The growing interest in Gaelic education in central Scotland and the greater variety of Gaelic teaching posts in these areas have resulted in rural and island vacancies being difficult to fill, since most young graduates choose to start their teaching career in a city or town rather than re-locate or return to rural areas. Some of the issues of isolation, identified in the previous section, can contribute to a graduate's reluctance to take up a teaching post in a rural or island location. Newly qualified teachers need the reassurance of collegial support that can usually only be found in larger Gaelic-medium units. Furthermore, few newly qualified teachers would relish the prospect of being the sole teacher in a composite Gaelic-medium setting.

This staffing and recruitment crisis has caused local authorities like Highland Council and Argyll and Bute Council to look at innovative ways of addressing acute staff shortages. In a unique partnership between the education services of Highland Council, Argyll and Bute Council, Comhairle nan Eilean Siar and the University of the Highlands and Islands Millenium Institute (UHIMI), a bursary scheme has been established to help support students from these three council areas to take up any full-time UHIMI Gaelic courses which offer a pathway to a career in Gaelic-medium teaching.

Argyll and Bute Council, in collaboration with Argyll College, has established a dedicated Gaelic immersion course for qualified teachers on Mull who wish to improve their Gaelic language skills in order to pursue careers within the GME sector. A funding package was secured from CNAG and SEED. Three teachers have recently completed the first year of their studies and have embarked on the second year of an immersion course that will give them the language skills necessary for successful Gaelic-medium teaching.

While commendable, the measures which address staff shortages and recruitment problems in the short term only paper over cracks to conceal what is a national staffing crisis. Those working in GME in 1986 never imagined that 16 years later there would still not be a dedicated Gaelic-medium pre-service teacher education course, despite countless campaigns to impress upon the powers-that-be that immediate action was necessary. How can we hope to attract suitably qualified and confident Gaelic teachers into the profession when we fail to afford them their minimum entitlement? The very least that Gaelic-medium teachers of the future deserve is the right to be trained in their native tongue. The Scottish Executive should be encouraged to act immediately and implement the recommendations contained within the GTCS report on GME if there is to be any hope of halting the decline in numbers pursuing careers in GME and any further Gaelic education developments in the future.

Pupil Integration and Inclusion

Another challenge facing a number of headteachers of Gaelic-medium establishments is the issue of pupil integration and inclusion. Headteachers should be committed to providing a progressive education for all children and young persons, appropriate to their age, abilities and aptitudes in a setting where students are valued and safe.

In recent years Scottish schools have embraced the key principles of inclusion and equal entitlement, yet GME remains 'ghettoised' in units within educational establishments. References to 'mainstream' and 'Gaelic-medium Units' give the impression that Gaelic is different from the norm and, as such, should be set apart. One would hope that, after 17 years of successful development, GME has itself become 'mainstream'. As we have mentioned, the decision made by many local authorities to remove the nomenclature Gaelic-medium units was a conscious effort to 'normalise' Gaelic education. Local authorities with Gaelic-medium provision positively encouraged integration so that Gaelic provision is not regarded as being 'a school within a school'.

Levels of integration can vary from school to school. However, one would expect Gaelic-medium classes to share the same school uniform, facilities and resources. More has to be done to break down the artificial barrier between English-medium and Gaelic-medium classes. If English-medium pupils learned some Gaelic or participated in joint projects on Scottish/Gaelic history and culture, children might perceive Gaelic as a language for life and not just for the classroom. Children should be afforded opportunities to work and play together and other languages, including Gaelic, should permeate whole-school activities such as assemblies, concerts and drama events. School management should decide how best to deploy Gaelic-medium staff in the light of the total pupil roll of the school, ensuring equal access to specialist staff for all pupils. It is important that Gaelic-medium pupils have access to whole school activities and contribute to the school ethos.

An example of best practice within the context of the secondary school can be found in Tobermory High School on Mull. The High School staff and pupils prepare for the transfer of Gaelic-medium pupils from Salen Primary into the High School by learning more about the benefits of bilingualism. Staff development seminars on *The Bilingual Learner* take place. Pupils participate in a *Languages Open Day* and everyone acquires a greater understanding of the cognitive benefits of bilingualism. Non-Gaelic-speaking teachers encourage bilingual pupils in their classes to discuss aspects of their work with Gaelic-speaking peers. Every lesson acknowledges the bilingual learners' right to access elements of their curriculum through Gaelic.

In 1999 Argyll and Bute Education Service instigated the Gaelic Language in the Primary School (GLPS) project. Similar GLPS provision is also available in areas of the Highland Council. This initiative, modelled on the national Modern Languages in the Primary School (MLPS) programme, involves training class teachers to teach Gaelic lessons to pupils in their own establishments. Teachers are given a 20-day intensive language learning experience and are provided with the resources necessary to deliver Gaelic language and culture to primary pupils.

GLPS is an ideal way of promoting Gaelic learning and teaching in schools with Gaelic-medium provision. While GLPS is intended to focus on language development at P6 and P7, it can be started much earlier. GLPS gives headteachers of Gaelic-medium provision the opportunity to develop Gaelic throughout their establishments, thus breaking down the feelings of many Gaelic-medium pupils that Gaelic is only a classroom language. The more teachers and pupils throughout the school who have knowledge of Gaelic language and culture the more likely it will be that the school climate will be one of tolerance and inclusion.

In 2001, while Minister for Education, Europe and External Affairs, Jack McConnell, giving the keynote address at the launch of the Action Group for Languages Recommendations for Modern Languages, paved the way for Gaelic to be perceived as every pupil's entitlement. In his address he stated that Scottish Gaelic is one of the many community languages that 'should be taught as a first modern language'.

There is no doubt that the numbers accessing GME alone will not be sufficient to revitalise the language and re-dress the decline in the number of Gaelic speakers. This is a view shared by many parents who feel that GLPS is an obvious alternative model to the Gaelic-medium option.

There has been a debate in the letters page of an Edinburgh evening paper recently supporting greater access to Gaelic language and culture in all Scottish schools. One correspondent claimed that: 'North of the central belt, legislation to promote Gaelic is taking hold and already many jobs require knowledge of Gaelic. This is very divisive in a country the size of Scotland. There should be a level playing-field with Gaelic available for everyone' (Ferguson, 2002). This is a view shared by Herald columnist, Jacky Kemp. She claims that the Gaelic-medium lobbyists are threatening the future of Gaelic. In her view, for Gaelic to survive a way must be found to '. . . open it up to the nation's children. It has to be a heritage that every Scot can lay claim to or it will not survive' (Kemp, 2002). The language learning model that GLPS offers can enhance existing Gaelic-medium developments and increase the number of young people being exposed to Gaelic language and culture.

Methodological Challenges

The methodological challenges shared by most bilingual Gaelic-medium teachers are likely to include:

- teaching small, composite classes with a diversity of learning needs;
- dealing with the shortage of a range of quality graded and differentiated teaching materials;
- dealing with the shortage of Gaelic-speaking support service staff to assist with pupils who have specific learning and behavioural difficulties;
- coping with the terminology, lexis and orthographic conventions associated with specific areas of the curriculum such as Science, Maths and Personal and Social Education;
- achieving an appropriate balance between oral fluency and the acquisition of idiomatic Gaelic and grammatical correctness.

The previous section highlighted the fact that most newly qualified teachers feel ill-prepared for the demands of Gaelic-medium classes because of the inadequate pre-service training courses offered by the teacher education institutions. The responsibility of supporting these newly qualified teachers once they enter the profession rests firmly with their local authorities. It is essential that appropriate support mechanisms be put in place to address teachers' needs when problems arise.

Coping with the Immersion Phase: issues of geographical location

GME involves the use of Gaelic language for all learning and teaching for all subjects in the curriculum. This is commonly termed the immersion method and is employed in the early stages of primary. The problems faced by immersion teachers can vary depending on whether they are teaching in the Highlands and Islands or the Lowland areas of Scotland.

Teachers in the Western Isles and areas in the Highland Council can experience problems with pitching the language in immersion classes at an appropriate level for the mixture of fluent speakers and complete beginners in their classes. These teachers fear that more English than Gaelic is spoken in their classrooms as they grapple with the diverse needs of those children with little or no Gaelic while still being aware of the needs of those who are fluent. The fluent speakers often prefer to speak English, which is the predominant language of the playground. This is not a phenomenon unique to GME as research has shown that it also prevails amongst children in *Irish Medium Education* (Hickey, 1997).

Teachers in central belt Gaelic-medium immersion classes are likely to have to cope with a mixture of native speakers, total beginners and speakers of Gaelic as a second language. The language which pupils bring with them to school depends on the language of their homes, whether one, both or neither parent speak Gaelic. Whether they have been to Gaelic pre-school and exposed to some Gaelic can influence the language competence of immersion pupils.

In 1996 Stradling and MacNeil reported that Gaelic-medium teachers use a wide range of teaching methods. These methods were drawn from the 1993 *National Guidelines for Curriculum and Assessment in Scotland: Gaelic 5–14* and research papers on bilingualism. Methodological issues common to virtually all immersion Gaelic-medium teachers include:

- creating positive classroom climates where learners enjoy learning Gaelic;
- supporting Gaelic speech with mime and gestures;
- using Gaelic-English inter-lingua while establishing Gaelic as the predominant medium for instruction;
- supporting and extending Gaelic vocabulary with songs, repetition and rhyme;

- developing topic-based learning opportunities that are relevant to the pupil's experiences.

Reaching the Bilingual Phase

English reading and writing skills will be introduced once pupils have attained Level A in national test items for reading and writing in Gaelic and usually by the end of primary three. Teachers will be expected to ensure a balanced approach to Gaelic and English reading homework tasks. To achieve *'broadly equal competence in Gaelic and English, in all the skills, by the end of primary seven'* (SOED,1993) both languages are likely to be used in primary 4 to primary 7 for teaching and learning. Gaelic will continue to be the predominant language of the bilingual classroom.

Information from teachers suggests that existing Gaelic-medium staff would welcome in-service training and support which focuses on strategies to address the methodological challenges highlighted at the start of this section. Stòrlann Nàiseanta na Gàidhlig can provide support with terminology and orthography by running courses specifically for Gaelic-medium teachers when new teaching materials are being launched. With appropriate levels of funding, Stòrlann might also be able to address the acute shortage of teaching materials for upper stage pupils.

One major concern is that GME will be unable to make further developments unless action is taken to ensure that new graduates entering the profession are adequately prepared to face the specific demands of a Gaelic-medium classroom. Newly qualified Gaelic-medium teachers will continue to raise the same concerns as those identified by existing teachers unless a dedicated Gaelic-medium pre-service training course is introduced which will address all the needs of our Gaelic teachers of the future.

The Role of Parents and the Community

The Chinese sage Lao Tzu once wrote:

> *Go to the people*
> *Live among them*
> *Start with what they know*
> *And when the deed is done*
> *The mission accomplished*
> *Of all the best leaders*
> *The people will say*
> *We did it*
> *Ourselves*

Lao Tzu might have had parents who have chosen Gaelic education for their children in mind when he wrote these words, for the growth of GME can largely be credited to parental power. It was parents who lobbied local authority representatives to investigate the feasibility of establishing Gaelic-medium provision in sixty locations across Scotland. It was parents who convinced local authorities that sufficient, sustainable demand for Gaelic education existed in these sixty locations. And it is parents who consistently support the efforts of teaching staff in developing the language competence of their children.

As mentioned in chapter one, in 1984 a parental group, CNP, was established in Inverness to lobby support for GME. This group was instrumental in securing funding for the first Gaelic-medium provision in Highland Council in 1986. As new Gaelic-medium provision was established so too were associated CNP groups, and there are now 32 constituted groups across Scotland. The groups represent the interests of parents whose children are being educated through the medium of Gaelic and usually complement the work of the School Board and the Parent/Teacher Associations in Gaelic Medium schools.

Like any other parent, those parents who chose Gaelic-medium provision are themselves the primary educators of their children. Whether Gaelic-speaking or not, parents can support and enhance the language development of their children in the home and in the wider community. If Gaelic is spoken in the home, children can extend their language skills through the acquisition of new vocabulary, idiom and register. Non-Gaelic speaking parents can support their children by creating a Gaelic ethos within the home. Schools can support parents in their efforts by supplying resources such as tapes and homework prompts. Parents can also draw on the support of the media and ensure their children have access to a range of Gaelic television and radio broadcasts. Comataigh Crolaidh Gàrdalig (CCG), the Gaelic Broadcasting Committee, has made a valuable contribution to the Gaelic renaissance by 'normalising' Gaelic programmes on TV and increasing the number of hours of Gaelic education programmes broadcast on TV and radio. It is clear that GME alone will not guarantee the survival of Gaelic language and culture. Young Gaelic speakers must have opportunities outwith their school settings to use their Gaelic in contexts where they feel confident and not self-conscious.

The national Gaelic agency, CNAG, has made an important contribution to the development of Gaelic language and culture. CNAG has played a strategic role in the development of Gaelic education, supporting local authorities in achieving their objectives. CNAG has also raised awareness of the economic opportunities associated with Gaelic and worked tirelessly to promote opportunities for youngsters to further develop their language skills in a variety of different extra-curricular activities and events. The Sradagan (Gaelic Youth Club) movement is an example of a CNAG-initiated project which supports young people in a range of extra-curricular sporting and musical activities through the medium of Gaelic.

Young people can participate in cultural activities through Fèisean (non-competitive music workshops) and local and National Mods (competitive Gaelic language and music festivals). Fèisean nan Gàidheal has supported the establishment of Fèisean in local areas throughout Scotland. These workshops help youngsters in GME become involved in cultural activities which will broaden their language experiences. These activities contribute to the Gaelic support network which is so essential for parents and pupils alike. Parents and children need to have opportunities to extend their Gaelic usage in meaningful contexts for Gaelic will not survive in a vacuum. A national strategy that plans for arts and culture and educational developments is necessary to maintain the momentum of growth and increase the number of Gaelic speakers.

Conclusion

This chapter has covered a wide range of issues, positions and strategies associated with the management of Gaelic-medium provision in schools but it has been by no means comprehensive. The picture emerging is that GME cannot sustain growth in isolation. A comprehensive, Scottish Executive-supported strategy is essential if the many needs identified in the previous sections are to be addressed and plans set in place for further developments. Strategic planning is essential to ensure the best use of limited Gaelic funding for the good of all associated with the regeneration of Gaelic.

CHAPTER 4

A LOCAL AUTHORITY PERSPECTIVE

Jean Nisbet

Introduction

National government, local authorities and community language groups have all played their part in the development of GME. It is important to note that enthusiasm for Gaelic has not been led exclusively by a single group. Local authorities and national government have worked closely with CNSA, CNAG, Clì — Na Gaidheil Ùra and CNP. All have been able to draw on the experience of language groups in other countries, such as Wales and Ireland, in determining the form that GME has taken over the past twenty years. Having together made great strides in the setting up of Gaelic-medium provision in the pre-school, primary and secondary sectors, all are now in a position, with the support of the newly formed Bòrd na Gàidhlig, to evaluate the progress of GME so far and to work together to resolve the great difficulties that still face GME: recruiting sufficient staff, developing GME in the secondary sector and exploring innovative approaches to ensure its future development.

The Main Partners

The partners have not always been willing allies. Community language groups complain that local and national government have shown a lack of enthusiasm for Gaelic language and culture. Local government has similarly complained that central government drags its feet on Gaelic issues. Local and national government have resigned themselves to never being seen to take the right line on Gaelic. Their motives are always suspect in the eyes of the language groups. Certainly, not all councillors and council taxpayers are enthusiasts for Gaelic education. Local politicians have sometimes found themselves caught between advocates for Gaelic and those hostile to Gaelic in the same council chamber.

The three groups have often disagreed in the past. A major source of contention was funding. The increase in enthusiasm for GME in the mid-

1980s coincided with a tough squeeze on local authority budgets by central government, with the result that pressure from community language groups to expand Gaelic education met with resistance from local authorities, who lacked the finance to meet the needs of parents seeking Gaelic education for their children. Gaelic education, with small numbers, high staffing ratios, transport costs inflated by the rural dimension and a serious deficit in teaching materials, was inherently more expensive than so-called mainstream education.

Once Gaelic Specific Grants came into existence in 1986, and Gaelic educational provision became more secure, community language groups and local and central government disagreed over the logistics of Gaelic provision. Where should it be sited? How should it be managed? Who should be eligible to enrol? Later came points of principle, much harder to resolve than mere money squabbles. There has never been agreement among the main players on priorities for Gaelic education. GME in primary schools has been able to command a large part of the budget simply because larger numbers of parents opt for Gaelic-medium primary education, but this has led to a neglect of secondary GME and learners in all sectors. Nor has there been any real discussion on the best form of GME which is most likely to produce children confident in both Gaelic and English. The immersion method, that is, teaching the curriculum only through Gaelic for at least the first two to three years of a child's formal schooling, has been the accepted way to proceed in Scotland, although that method is long overdue for review.

CNSA has frequently been a thorn in the flesh of some local authorities, but, overall, local government would concede that it made an outstanding contribution to Gaelic in the early years of the revival. CNSA raised parental awareness of the value of early Gaelic education and of self-help partnerships. It encouraged immersion at a time when this form of education was almost unknown in Scotland. It defied common sense by planting groups in west central Scotland, for example in Ayrshire and Renfrewshire, areas which, unlike Glasgow, do not have a visible resident Gaelic-speaking population, indeed where Gaelic has not been spoken for some four hundred years. Yet CNSA groups have flourished so well there that parents have been empowered to request the support of local authorities to the extent that their playgroups have developed into full-blown pre-school and primary units.

From its inception in 1984, CNAG demonstrated its willingness to work with other organisations and local and national government. CNAG's biggest difficulty has been that local government has never liked the idea of being at the command of an external agency. CNAG's role as a national organisation has resulted in a tension between its national responsibility for the development of Gaelic-medium education throughout Scotland and the statutory responsibility of local authorities for the general development of education within their own areas. The position of CLI has been an uneasy one until fairly recent times. Local authorities have had to make their priority the larger numbers of Gaelic native-speakers and parents of pupils in GME, with the result that learners of Gaelic have been largely ignored in budgetary terms. However, local authorities are aware that there are now more Gaelic learners in the community and council departments such as Community Support now work closely with CLI to devise imaginative approaches to working with learners. Primary schools also play their part by training non-Gaelic-speaking teachers to offer Gaelic language for the primary school alongside French or German, thus opening up access for all to Gaelic and integrating Gaelic into the school curriculum.

The relationship between the local authorities and CNP, both local branches and the national organisation, is more informal and often dependent on the personalities involved. Relationships have occasionally broken down, but parents with children in GME, some of whose experiences of lobbying go back to the first campaign for Gaelic-medium classes in the early 1980s, are skilled in their dealings with politicians and aware of the need to work with local authorities. Much of the community language groups' influence depends on the role they have in providing information on developments in the Gaelic world both to parents and to local authorities.

Gaelic Specific Grants

In 1982, CNES, Highland Regional Council and Strathclyde Regional Council together submitted to the Scottish Office a bid for specific grant funding to develop Gaelic education. The bid was rejected on the basis that specific grants, grants targeted at one 'ring-fenced' area, should be avoided wherever possible, since local authorities should be left with the freedom to allocate resources in accordance with their own perception of local needs.

Almost immediately, in 1984, the Scottish Office Montgomery Report included in its recommendations the proposal that specific grants should be created for Gaelic education. As its full title suggests, *Committee of Inquiry into the Functions and Powers of the Islands Councils of Scotland*, the main concerns of the Report were not Gaelic, Gaelic education or Gaelic-medium Education, but the right of local authorities to make decisions which uniquely affected their own population. The Montgomery Report put on paper the belief, already gaining ground among local authorities both in the central belt and in the Gaidhealtachd at the time, that 'the preservation, promotion and development of Gaelic should be a local authority function.' (Scottish Office, 1984, p.65). The report effectively provided the framework for GME development.

The Montgomery Report's recommendations led most obviously to the establishment of Gaelic Specific Grants in 1986. The argument of the writers of the Report was that there would be no harm in setting up specific grants for Gaelic, since 'Gaelic concerns only a small number of authorities.' (Scottish Office, 1984, p.67). The Report's writers could hardly have predicted the 'bandwagon' effect. Local authorities with an interest in Gaelic were already working together. With fluent speakers, learners, teachers and parents in contact with each other through a wide range of Gaelic organisations, there grew up, and very rapidly too, a demand for Gaelic education in more than just the local authorities where Gaelic was most commonly spoken.

Importantly, the Montgomery Report recognised the work which had been going on in CNES to establish a bilingual policy without additional financial support from central government. It accepted that support for Gaelic in the islands had its basis in the reality of economics: Gaelic might not necessarily directly benefit the local economy, but it would certainly give local people 'strengthened confidence' (Scottish Office, 1984, p.65) by preserving their culture and, as part of their culture, their language. The Report told central government, for the first time and in an inquiry that it had itself commissioned, that the preservation and promotion of Gaelic culture generally 'required a level of financial resources not needed elsewhere' (Scottish Office, 1984, p.65). It also recommended that this requirement be quantified. Moreover, also for the first time, the Report suggested that 'in (Gaelic) education, the level of additional resources required is particularly high'. The Report recommended that central government give up being 'reactive', merely responding 'to initiatives from Gaelic organisations'. Indeed, it went so far as to observe that its inquiry had found 'no concrete evidence of an explicit national policy'. It commented that 'Government support (for Gaelic) seems to be expressed largely in financial terms' (Scottish Office, 1984, all p.65) and proposed that 'some broad policy . . . be worked out by all interested bodies with agreed objectives and responsibilities clearly apportioned between local authorities, central government and agencies concerned' (Scottish Office, 1984, p.66). For the first time, national government was being urged to take the lead in Gaelic matters.

The Effects of Gaelic Specific Grants

By 2002–3, Gaelic Specific Grants for education stood at £2 million, having doubled in the previous five years. The advantages of Gaelic Specific Grants soon became clear to national government and to those local authorities with an interest in the provision of Gaelic education. The establishment of a system of bidding for finance from a centrally-held fund gave local authorities stability for the first time in their planning for Gaelic. Authorities could take a fairly long-term view of Gaelic development, secure in the knowledge that their local government contribution of 25% towards staffing, resources and equipment would be 'topped up' by a 75% contribution from the central scheme. For the first time, too, central government was in a position to direct the development of Gaelic education. A bidding system required local authorities to think out their future plans and to frame their developments in a bid that would meet the approval of central government. Very soon, a local authority group, IASG, was formed. At first, its members were council officers and representatives of CNAG and central government, but local politicians quickly replaced council officers, in itself, an indication of the importance of Gaelic in political terms. The Management Review Group, (MRG), made up of council officers and civil servants from the Scottish Office Education Department, and with representation from CNAG, was formed soon after, to oversee the development of the Gaelic curriculum and resources.

Under the direction of the MRG, various curriculum groups were formed, the Secondary Review Group, the Primary Review Group, the Community Education Review Group, with responsibility for the commissioning and writing of classroom materials. The groups met regularly and were often staffed by Gaelic-speaking council officers who produced a vast quantity of good teaching material.

However, the expansion of GME into the secondary and pre-school sectors meant, that by the mid-1990s, other more formal means of producing materials had to be sought. In 1999, Stòrlann Nàiseanta na Gàidhlig was established with a manager and a board made up of representatives of local authorities, Sabhal Mòr Ostaig and CNAG. Stòrlann provides a service to all sectors of Gaelic education, especially in co-ordinating the production and distribution of teaching materials in Gaelic. It is funded in two ways: a grant from the Scottish Executive pays for salaries and other costs associated with the running of Stòrlann, while funding from the Scheme of Specific Grants for Gaelic, via the local authorities, allows for the production of school resources. It is expected that all local authorities deriving a benefit from Stòrlann in terms of teaching materials will contribute a percentage of their total spend annually for the production of materials. The Stòrlann can also raise additional funds through publishing materials.

The main disadvantage of Gaelic Specific Grants is that some local authorities have clearly become dependent on central funding. In principle, local authorities are encouraged to absorb projects attracting Gaelic

Specific Grants into their own budgets within five years of the project's inception. In effect, this has not always happened. In some cases, local authorities have threatened to bring to an end projects established for more than ten years on the grounds that their poor financial health does not allow them to meet the full cost of running these projects.

If success can be reckoned by the number of Gaelic-medium establishments opened, the number of children enrolled and the number of local authorities making provision for Gaelic since the establishment of Gaelic Specific Grants in 1986, then local and central government in Scotland has served GME well. However, in retrospect, it is clear that the good intentions of the Montgomery Report were not going to meet all the challenges inherent in developing GME. Even with specific grants established by 1986, CNES, Highland Regional Council and Strathclyde Regional Council were not totally convinced that GME was the desirable provision. In Strathclyde, where a decision to set up a Gaelic-medium primary unit in Sir John Maxwell Primary School pre-dated the creation of Gaelic Specific Grants, there was still considerable doubt as to the wisdom of the decision, with some politicians, council officers and parents far from convinced that the establishment of a Gaelic unit was the best use to make of funding. For those living in council areas where Gaelic was not seen as a living community language, parents and other advocates for Gaelic had a struggle to persuade local authorities to apply for specific grants and had no mechanism to force councils to do so. From the point of view of educators charged with establishing Gaelic-medium schools and classes, the lack of resources in the Gaelic language has been a constant difficulty. In addition, while local authorities are expected to set aside 10% of their total Gaelic budget for the provision of resources, there is no means of ensuring that they do so. Overall, then, the approach to GME that grew up after 1986 was in essence *ad hoc*. Decisions were often taken in haste, without adequate research and preparation.

Gaelic Immersion

The form of GME implemented by the Strathclyde and Highland Regional Councils in 1985 and by CNES in 1986 was the immersion system. Children entering Primary 1 arrived in a classroom where only Gaelic was spoken. Gaelic was the language children learned to read first. They covered every aspect of the curriculum through the medium of Gaelic for all of Primary 1 and 2 and for part of Primary 3. Gradually, in the course of Primary 3, English was introduced as a subject taught in English and then, as children went through Primary 4 to 7, other aspects of the curriculum were dealt with through English, until by Primary 7 children were used to working for part of each day in Gaelic and part in English. The advantages of this system were obvious. A child with no background in Gaelic entering Primary 1 went into a world where everything was new. Gaelic was part of the new experience and children, at their most receptive in language terms between birth and age seven, accepted the language along with the rest of the curriculum. Making Gaelic the first language of the classroom demonstrated the value that the teacher and other adults working with the children placed on the Gaelic language. Immersion gave the children constant exposure to Gaelic in the early stages of primary, which compensated to an extent for the absence of Gaelic in some children's homes and families. The ingenuity of teachers in devising methods of instruction and materials for learning meant that there were remarkably few drop outs.

Research (Johnstone, 1999) indicates that parents' faith in Gaelic Medium by immersion is rewarded. In the early years of their primary education, children and their teachers carry a considerable curriculum load, but, by the end of Primary 7, children educated through Gaelic immersion have caught up with and in some cases overtaken their peers in English language classes.

Gaelic Bilingualism

It is worth noting that the form of GME first introduced in CNES after regionalisation in 1975 was bilingual education. It attempted to give equal value to English and Gaelic in the classroom. Pupils accessed part of the curriculum through the medium of Gaelic from the start of their education. For example, the Expressive Arts or Environmental Studies might be offered through Gaelic. The percentage of classroom time given over to lessons through Gaelic was gradually increased over the seven years of primary education. The intention was always that, by Primary 7, children would be as comfortable in Gaelic as they were in English.

Bilingualism is the preferred language model in many parts of the United States, as extensively researched and reported on by Thomas and Collier (1997). They have followed the education of several thousand children for up to twenty-five years from their arrival in elementary school as monolingual speakers of Spanish or Korean into their adult lives. Their research indicates that results will only ensue from bilingual education for the 'minority' language if what are perceived within Western education as the 'serious' parts of the curriculum, Maths and language, are presented through the minority language. (Ironically, the highly-respected bilingual model is now under attack in California, where the state legislature's Proposition 227 seeks to abandon the bilingual model in favour of an 'English only' education for its immigrant population. No evaluation of the effects on children of the loss of bilingual education has yet been carried out). The CNES model offered language and Maths through the medium of English and other areas of the curriculum through Gaelic. In the early 1980s, the CNES experiment was slow to produce results. It did not, in any case, run long enough for the results to be scientifically evaluated and parents began to agitate for the immersion model described above, which was then under discussion in Highland and Strathclyde regions.

Decisions taken at the origins of GME, in response to parental demand or as a reaction to a political impetus or to a sense of urgency to get something in place quickly, have denied innovators in Gaelic education time to reflect on the work in hand. Long-term planning for growth was also noticeably absent. This has, in turn, led to a narrowing of the range of innovative approaches in education during the current revival. Teachers and parents were aware that they were involved in something new but they did not want experiments to devise the 'best' model for Gaelic, but a form of education that mirrored what children got in English-language classes.

The Growth of Gaelic Medium Education

Gaelic-medium teaching using the immersion method has had relative success between 1985 and 2000. The number of primary units and number of pupils enrolled have steadily increased. The latest figures indicate that there are 60 Gaelic-medium primary units in 14 local authorities: Aberdeen City, Angus, Argyll & Bute, Edinburgh, East Ayrshire, East Dunbartonshire, Glasgow, Highland, Inverclyde, North Lanarkshire, Perth and Kinross, South Lanarkshire, Stirling and Comhairle nan Eilean Siar. The growth in the number of Gaelic-medium primary units can be seen in Table 6 and the steady rise in the number of pupils enrolled in Gaelic-medium primary classes is illustrated in Table 1 (page 13).

The widespread development of pre-school education (see Table 7) in the 1990s in Scotland is reflected in the number of local authority Gaelic nursery places available by 2000 in 33 nurseries in 12 local authorities: Aberdeen City, Argyll & Bute, East Ayrshire, East Dunbartonshire, Edinburgh City, Glasgow City, Highland, Inverclyde, North Lanarkshire, Perth & Kinross, South Lanarkshire, CNES. These local authority nurseries exist side-by-side with 125 CNSA pre-school groups involving 1900 children.

Gaelic-medium secondary provision is in place in 13 centres in 4 local authorities: Argyll & Bute, Glasgow, Highland and Comhairle nan Eilean Siar. The Gaelic-medium secondary population is shown in Table 8.

Local Authority Support for GME

The development of a system of GME by immersion, which can be used in any establishment in any local authority, has meant a major change in thinking for local government. Gaelic has never been the domain of the handful of local authority areas where Gaels are to be found in large number but is a target for parents in any local authority, both those from a Gaelic-speaking background and those with little or no experience of Gaelic but an enthusiasm for the language and culture. Of the twenty-two local authorities in receipt of Gaelic Specific Grants, fourteen offer GME. The other eight authorities will argue that their Gaelic priorities lie elsewhere, for example, in meeting the demands of adult learners. Ten local authorities make no Gaelic provision at all. In these cases there may be a lack of demand for Gaelic, but it is well known among Gaelic speakers that some local authorities refuse to consider Gaelic provision for a variety of reasons. After the re-organisation of local government in 1996, some authorities lacked funding to make the 25% local authority contribution needed for Gaelic Specific Grants. Others found themselves without the personnel and the expertise to support Gaelic provision.

Pre-school provision

Local authority nurseries provide some Gaelic input and some local provision at pre-school level is provided by the CNSA, but there are major gaps in Gaelic pre-school provision. Local authorities need support at national level to fill gaps there for those parents who wish it and a more strategic and less haphazard approach can only be of benefit to Gaelic. The best way to recruit children to Gaelic-medium primary classes is to have a Gaelic nursery in the same school building.

Destination of Primary 7 pupils

This is one of the most serious problems facing Gaelic education. Children educated from Croileagan (Playgroup) to Primary 7 have a rich experience of Gaelic language and culture. Thanks to the Gaelic-medium system of immersion, they are quickly fluent in Gaelic. They learn Gaelic music and poetry, Gaelic stories and folklore. To become fluent adolescents and then adults, they need to continue with their education, with their participation at Sradagan (Gaelic youth clubs), with their involvement in feisean and in all the other experiences which will produce in them a fully-developed command of Gaelic for adulthood. Many parents seem to make the decision to move their children into 'mainstream' education at the end of their primary schooling. It would be interesting to know their reasons, and thus discover whether local authorities and

Gaelic community organisations can do more to convince them to stay within the Gaelic system.

It would certainly help the status of Gaelic in schools generally if the present distinction between learners and fluent speakers were to disappear, to be replaced in Scottish Qualifications Authority examinations by a system of assessment that accepts that many young people now in Gaelic-medium Education are learners to some extent and gauges their progress on a learning continuum.

The failure of Gaelic-medium secondary education to pick up pupils can be seen firstly in the erratic figures for Gaelic at Standard Grade and Higher, both Native Speakers and Learners (cf Table 9). The poor uptake in the Standard Grade examinations available through the medium of Gaelic in History, Geography and Mathematics tells a similar story. Between 1993 and 2001, no pupil sat Standard Grade Maths in Gaelic, in only four of those years did pupils sit Geography and only History presented pupils for S Grade through Gaelic in each of those years. The questions to be asked here are why so few secondary pupils sat these Standard Grades through the medium of Gaelic and how many pupils embarked on a course, only to give it up before completion because of the shortage of teachers or resources.

Issues in Gaelic Medium Education

Research
Research in education fulfils two functions: quality assurance and the dissemination of good practice. This is especially important in Gaelic education, where practitioners and local authority officers sometimes work in relative isolation. Local authorities working in GME are acutely aware of the lack of information gleaned from solid academic and practitioner research, both about GME and about other types of immersion and bilingual education, about children's responses to these types of education and, of great importance to local authorities, the experience and views of teachers working in GME.

Gaelic Staffing — and how it affects Parental Choice
Not all teachers are prepared to consider working in GME, especially in rural areas which do not always attract young teachers. Some teachers opt in but regret doing so and may opt out very quickly. They fear they will be professionally trapped because GME is perceived to have a narrow focus. It also has limited career prospects because of an absence of promoted posts. Working as a Gaelic-medium teacher has also tended to be more onerous in the past. For a long time there was a dearth of good resources, with the result that Gaelic-medium teachers, classroom assist-

ants and parents were obliged to spend a lot of time 'pasting up', that is, covering over the English text in school books with Gaelic translations. The need to do this amateurish adaptation increased the sense of Gaelic being the poor relation in educational terms. There are also clear pressures attached to working in a language that is not the principal language of the school (most Gaelic classes operate alongside English classes), but not enough information is available to inform local authorities of the views of staff who work in this setting.

Nor is enough research available to give parents the information they need when making decisions with their children about their future education. Part of the credit for the spread of GME at the primary stage must go to organisations such as CNP and CNAG but research is also needed to answer parents' questions. At the secondary stage is the Gaelic experience sustainable at all? Is the focus of Gaelic-medium secondary education currently so narrow that it is perceived to be pointless in some cases? How many subjects taught through the medium of Gaelic are necessary to produce a young person with a wide and mature grasp of the Gaelic language? Can a wider range of subjects be taught through the medium of Gaelic, given the teacher shortage?

Many of the doubts expressed by parents are linked to the fact that local authorities experience difficulty in recruiting staff for GME. The establishment of the Stòrlann Nàiseanta na Gàidhlig is rapidly giving teachers access to high-quality resources for GME, but, in matters of staffing, local authorities have found that the demand outstrips the supply of suitable professionals, including teachers, supply staff, speech therapists, psychologists, classroom assistants and other support workers

It is to the credit of those working in the Gaelic-medium sector that Gaelic education is distinguished by being socially inclusive to a degree that might be envied by 'mainstream' education. However, if GME is to continue to make appropriate provision for children with special educational needs, a way must be found to secure the services of professionals who will make this possible. In-service tutors who will be able to provide professional development for staff in the Gaelic sector are also required.

Rural local authorities in particular report difficulty in attracting and retaining teachers. Even in the central belt, traditionally an attractive area for Gaelic-speaking teachers, it has happened that a local authority has only been able to fill a gap in its staffing by recruiting a teacher from the Gaelic-medium class of a neighbouring authority, leaving an unbridgeable gap in provision there.

In 2002, encouraging attempts to overcome problems of teacher supply have led firstly to the creation of a teacher education initiative involving Lews Castle College and Strathclyde University. This scheme hopes to overcome the shortage of Gaelic-speaking teachers in the islands by allowing them to train locally, using a mixed method of delivery: locally-based training combined with the use of ICT (e-mail, internet, whiteboard and video-conferencing) to bring the trainers virtually to the learners. Secondly, Argyll and Bute has opted to recruit teachers already in its schools who wish to train in Gaelic and provide Gaelic immersion education locally. These teachers continue to work in schools in their communities while participating in distance-learning Gaelic courses through Argyll College. Aberdeen University in partnership with Highland Council is preparing a two-year part-time PGCE course which can be delivered by distance learning.

Central Government
The creation of the Scottish Parliament has made parliamentarians more accessible to their constituents and community Gaelic organisations. Since 1997, Gaelic has been part of the Scottish Executive's National Priorities for Education. The third of the five priorities states this aim under the heading of inclusion and equality: 'to promote equality and help every pupil benefit from education with particular regard paid to pupils with disabilities and special educational needs, and to Gaelic and other lesser used languages'. It will be interesting to see whether the eight local authorities with no Gaelic school provision will be expected to include the school sector in their future development. It will also be interesting to see whether the ten authorities with no Gaelic provision at all are persuaded to become involved. Similarly, if GME is to be considered a success, ways must be found to allow pupils a wider experience than just Gaelic and one other secondary subject through the medium of Gaelic, the main secondary provision available at the moment. Young people and their parents are entitled to ask if inclusion in the National Priorities for Education means anything or if a minimum entitlement needs to be included in the definition of Gaelic provision.

One of the major difficulties for local authorities in developing Gaelic provision is the misplacing of Gaelic education in the Arts and Cultural Heritage section of the Scottish Executive, rather than in the Education section. Gaelic does, of course, have a role to play in the arts and cultural heritage of Scotland and it has a claim to a considerable part of that budget as an increasingly important source of tourism revenue for the country. But Gaelic education needs to be considered alongside mainstream education. It will only achieve parity when it is a responsibility of the Education portfolio, considered side-by-side with English language pre-school, primary and secondary education. Isolated in Arts and Cultural Heritage, Gaelic education is put in the position of having to remind those working on new projects of its existence and of its claim to a share of the funding available.

Within the Scottish Executive Education Department, Gaelic desperately needs a voice: as far back as 1984, the Montgomery Report described the need for a central body to oversee the development of the language and, more recently, both the MacPherson and the Meek Reports (2000 and 2002) have given such a measure their support. The development of GME is crucial to the continuing revival of Gaelic: if GME is to maintain the quality of the educational experience it offers while it continues to expand, it will need the support of a body capable of taking an overview of developments in Gaelic generally and of providing direction and long-term planning to those who work in the field.

The Future for Gaelic

Gaelic is not immune from the changes facing education and Scottish society in general. If GME can be considered to have got off to a good start in the final decades of the twentieth century, thanks to the alliance of national government, local authorities and community language groups, then the next twenty years are likely to see more rapid development at national and local levels. The establishment of Bòrd na Gàidhlig is of the most obvious significance for GME. The creation of the Bòrd puts Gaelic in its strongest position ever in Scotland. It may be that secure status for Gaelic will follow immediately, but, whatever happens, expectations are high. Local authorities facing the demand from Gaels, old and new, for a lifelong experience of Gaelic will look to the Bòrd to put together a policy which will encourage a sense of community in a scattered Gaelic-speaking population with a wide range of experiences.

It may be that, twenty years after the Montgomery Report, Gaels are about to acquire in Bòrd na Gàidhlig that 'central body' whose 'positive guidance and support . . . would be beneficial' to local authorities. Local authority politicians and officers, parents, children and learners will all hope to see that the good start made in recent years will be built on.

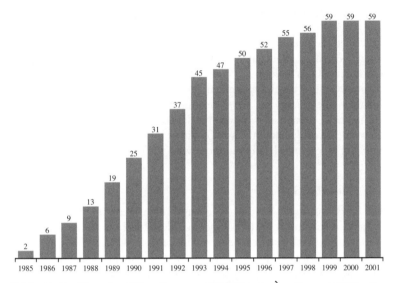

Table 6: Foghlam tro Mheadhan na Gàidhlig aig Ìre Bun-sgoile/*Gaelic-medium Primary Education* **1985–2001 Àireamh Aonadan/Number of Units**

Table 7: Foghlam Sgoil Àraich tro Mheadhan na Gàidhlig *Gaelic-medium Nursery Education* **1993–2001 Àireamh Cloinne/***Number of Pupils*

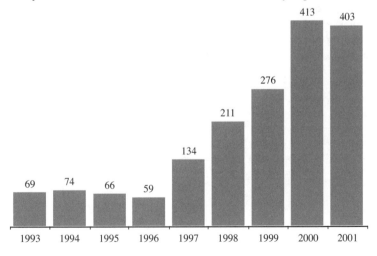

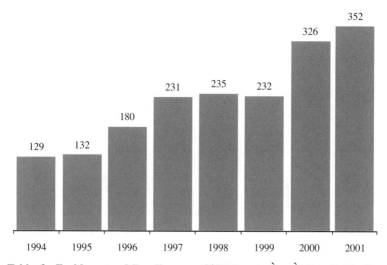

Table 8: Foghlam tro Mheadhan na Gàidhlig aig Ìre Àrd-sgoile/*Gaelic-medium Secondary Education* 1994–2001 Àireamh Sgoilearan/*Number of Pupils*

Table 9: Gàidhlig mar Chuspair san Àrd-sgoil/*Gaelic as a Subject in the Secondary School* Àireamh a' Suidhe Dheuchainnean/*Number of Presentations*

Standard Grades

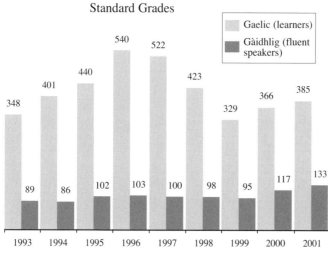

Year

Standard Grades

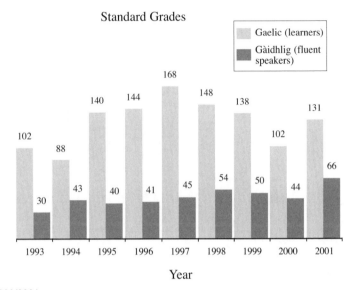

Year

2000/2001

2,310 pupils studying Gaelic (Learners) in 34 Secondary Schools (S1–S6)

899* pupils studying Gàidhlig (Fluent Speakers) in 32 Secondary Schools (S1–S6)

*Includes the 326 pupils following Gaelic-medium Secondary Education

Advanced Higher: Learners – 11; Fluent Speakers – 11; CSYS – 9 > total of 31 at level

13 of Scottish Credit and Qualification Framework

CHAPTER 5

CONTEXTS AND FUTURES

Margaret Nicolson and Matthew MacIver

Introduction

In the preceding chapters it becomes clear that the development and the present situation and status of Gaelic Medium Education, like that of the Gaelic language itself, can be better understood when the contexts in which it is set are made clear. Issues linked to the broader linguistic, educational and political contexts emerge, for the status and development of GME is also reliant upon them. For example, an assumption that language medium education is worth pursuing is predicated on the belief that value is assigned to the maintenance of a multilingual world and, therefore, to the promotion of language and language education in all its forms as an important part of the social and educational fabric. If we are gaining the view that Scotland has been less than enthusiastic about the need for GME it is to these contexts we must also turn for explanation.

The Linguistic Context

Three main areas for discussion emerge in the linguistic context: the domination of a monolingual culture in Scotland, the place of language in the identity discussion in Scotland and the particular case of the Gaelic language within Scotland.

In Scotland, as in many English-speaking contexts, a monolingual culture has dominated for a long time. Although Scotland behaves as a monolingual country its linguistic reality can be constructed in quite a different way if we choose to assume a different perspective (Nicolson, 2000). As well as English and the indigenous languages of Gaelic and Scots (in all its variants), Scotland also has a number of community languages such as Urdu, Ukrainian, Italian, Cantonese, Polish and Punjabi, to name but a few. Indeed, MacKinnon's work (1994) on the 1991 census figures on ethnic origin estimated that around 95,000 people in Scotland spoke a language *other* than English, Scots or Gaelic as their first language. Yet, a multilingual environment, of the sort we find in some European countries, Belgium, Switzerland, or parts of Italy and Spain, for example, where several languages, majority and/or minority ones co-exist relatively happily, with some speakers using several in the course of a day, is relatively rare here. In Scotland, when there is a concentration of bilingualism or multilingualism, this tends to be in specific geographic areas such as the Gaelic heartland of the Western Isles, or in specific community groups, such as the Cantonese–speaking communities in Edinburgh and Glasgow. Although many monolingual Scots may be in daily contact with bilinguals at work, at school or socially, their experience of language interaction with them is likely to be in English, since the bilinguals' other language will be reserved for family and/or community settings. It is fair to add that bilingualism or multi-lingualism has tended to be viewed in Scotland, as in other English-dominant cultures, as different from the norm. It could be argued that the fact we feel obliged to attach epithets, such as 'foreign', 'heritage' and 'community' to different categories of language is indicative of more than simply a desire to be descriptive: these epithets can perpetuate feelings about the supremacy of the dominant language, which carries no such epithet; they can create a sense of a linguistic difference rather than linguistic diversity and they can reinforce an artificial hierarchy of language rather than bolster a diverse array, each of equal worth in linguistic if not socio-political terms.

Another key factor in the linguistic context, as McLeod has pointed out in chapter two, and in direct relation to a strong monolingual culture, is the absence in Scotland of a clear link between language and identity. Language per se has not traditionally figured as a primary component of how individuals in Scotland view themselves or how they are viewed by officialdom. The census does not seek to find out, for example, the mother tongue of all respondents in order to gain a language picture of the population. Although Gaelic does receive attention in the census the 'Gaelic question' is limited and open to ambiguity. It does not ask respondents whether Gaelic is the mother tongue language, whether they are bilingual in Gaelic and another language, or whether they are learning or are fluent in the language, but to tick discrete boxes indicating whether they can either speak, read write or understand Gaelic. This inevitably gives a different type of picture based on discrete language skills rather than a holistic view, although a holistic view of the number of speakers is nonetheless based on these answers.

The link between language and Scottish national identity poses diffi-culty since Scotland has not been a linguistically unified entity in historic terms. It can be argued that only where language becomes a distinct marker of identity, when there is a grasp of the difference 'between language in its ordinarily understood sense as a tool of communication, and language as an emblem of groupness, as a symbol, a rallying point' (Edwards, 1985, p.17) does it receive greater focus both from the individual and from the group or community. Gaelic, as a so-called 'heritage language', falls into that category. As MacDonald has written: 'heritage languages are seen to lie at the heart of a deep-seated identity . . . language use is conceptualised not so much as a pragmatic matter as an affective, symbolic and political one; the decline in 'a people's language' is seem as evidence of alienation and perhaps even repression. The loss of a heritage language is synonymous with the loss of identity.' (Macdonald 1997, p.219). A recent survey among some HE students in Scotland (Nicolson, forthcoming) seems to confirm this view. The bilingual Gaelic-English respondents rated language and the associated factors of culture and community more highly in a set of identity factors than did the monolinguals. Comments elucidating the reasons for their ratings indicated that they perceived language as a key component of who they are.

A further issue is the particularly isolated and lowly place in which the Gaelic language in Scotland has found itself. If languages generally are not highly valued in Scotland then Gaelic, like Scots, has been worse off than many others, finding itself at the bottom of the artificially imposed hierarchy. The historic roots are well known. Gaelic was seen as a cause of barbarity and lack of civility from the 17th century (Acts of 1616 and 1696). The Scottish Society for the Propagation of Christian Knowledge (SSPCK) deemed it an impediment to spiritual and moral progress (SSPCK Records, Letter and Minutes, 1707–1741). The Poor Law enquiry of 1844 viewed it as an impediment to economic and social progress (Withers, 1998, p.133). This view stems from what Baker terms the 'language as an obstacle' issue, where the minority language is connected to 'poverty, underachievement in school, minimal social and vocational mobility and with a lack of integration into the majority culture' (Baker, 1996, p.354). Although it has been tempting, and indeed sometimes necessary, to stress Gaelic's differences and the different needs of GME, such a position will tend to further rather than improve the isolationist context which has its roots deep in history. As long as the educational infrastructure continues to bolster rather than eradicate isolationism solutions will prove extremely difficult to identify.

The Educational Context

As a direct consequence of the linguistic context, the educational context has played its part in how language generally and Gaelic in particular have been perceived, which in turn has had an effect on how language medium education is perceived.

Firstly, the historical bias against Gaelic already mentioned receives tacit expression in the Education (Scotland) Act, 1872. There is indeed some merit to the argument that the 1872 Act accelerated a process of cultural erosion which has challenged the language ever since. The Act laid the foundation of an educational system for the Highlands which was to be in close conformity with that of the rest of the country. It offered no acceptance of the unique linguistic situation existing in the Highlands, and Gaelic as a language or as a means of delivery of education was given no recognition. Worse still, punishment for speaking Gaelic was rife in some schools in the latter part of the 19th century and early part of the 20th century. The general result was the alienation from their culture of successive generations of Gaelic speakers for whom devaluation of their language was implicit, and frequently made explicit, in their schooling.

Secondly, the place of languages in the Scottish curriculum has been distinctive. The teaching of languages, even as discrete subjects in Scottish schools, has, it is fair to say, had an elitist past. In the secondary school system, for example, languages were historically reserved beyond Secondary 2 for those with an apparent aptitude for them, unlike Maths, English, or the Social Sciences. The entry of languages into the compulsory core curriculum to 16 for all in the 1990s was not greeted with overwhelming joy on the part of the majority, some language teachers included, who wished to retain the elite label (Nicolson, 2000). The teaching of languages in primary school has only begun in the last decade under the Modern Languages in Primary School (MLPS) and the GLPS schemes. Provision is by no means uniform and articulation with secondary school is occasionally problematic as a result. Given this background, it is hardly surprising that the teaching of all subjects via another language might be a difficult one for many Scottish educationalists to accept, particularly if children entering language-medium education, as is the case with children from non-Gaelic-speaking homes entering GME, are not fluent in the language in which they are being educated or not deemed to be able linguists. Paradoxically, the same argument has not held historically regarding Gaelic speakers daily confronting a system where delivery is via English and not via their first language! Grant has talked about the historically prevalent '*deficit* model of bilingualism' perpetuated in Scotland and indeed the UK, where another language was thought to educationally disadvantage the child (Grant, 2000, p.30). However, things are beginning to change. Along with the growth in GME we have also seen the setting up of a French Medium project in Torry Primary School in Aberdeen. The report on attainment in GME mentioned in earlier chapters has also proved that children in GME are not being educationally disadvantaged. (Johnstone et al, 1999).

Thirdly, even within language education in Scotland, Gaelic has been set apart. For example, the delivery of Gaelic as a language subject and its departmental status within the school structure has been historically separate from modern language provision within the secondary school. The fact that native speakers and learners of the language have to be catered for has undoubtedly been one of the reasons for this separation. However, the separate nature of Gaelic language teaching has meant that methodological developments, fast-moving in the teaching of European languages since the 1960s, have been slower to come to teacher education in Gaelic and therefore to Gaelic delivery in the classroom. As a result, there has not been the same focus on the acquisition of communicative competence, which would be of particular benefit to non-native speakers who are learning the language or who are using the language as their learning medium in other subjects. The same has been the case in the adult language learning domain. Often, the repertoire of teaching techniques has proved to be more limited than in the 'foreign' language domain and the focus on certain aspects of acquisition (spoken fluency, intonation, pronunciation, for example) less than rigorous. One key reason is that those who teach in this domain are not necessarily language professionals and therefore not versed in language teaching skills.

Documentation and discussion on language methodology and language development have not traditionally included Gaelic, Scots and its variants, or community languages for that matter, and it is only fairly recently that debates about immersion methodology in GME are being engaged in by a wider audience than those directly involved in this area. A welcome break from this pattern was contained in the report from the Ministerial Action Group on Languages *Citizens of a Multilingual World* (SEED, 2000), which was inclusive of languages, foreign, heritage and community, within its remit. It also aimed to address what it termed the 'climate of negativity' surrounding languages which included negative attitudes, low motivation and high language anxiety. It felt that in Scotland 'social attitudes to languages are often confused and ambivalent'. However, does the reality of the political context in Scotland allow for initiatives such as GME to take flight? To what extent is the political context helping to reverse past educational and cultural legacies in this domain?

The Political Context

Scotland is a small country with a fairly tight and constrained system of education. There are two main reasons for this compactness. First of all, policy has traditionally been in the hands of a small group of people, ministers in the Scottish Executive, civil servants in Scotland and, previously, Her Majesty's Inspectors of Education (HMIE). Now that HMIE have lost their policymaking role, power is concentrated in even fewer hands. Secondly, in curricular terms, although Scotland has guidelines, previously prepared by the former Scottish Consultative Committee on the Curriculum (SCCC), rather than a national curriculum, the effect is still the same in that these guidelines are taken as the way to proceed. There is, then, little or no curricular autonomy for schools and very little room for manoeuvre for headteachers. In the primary sector, for example, the curriculum is dominated by the 5–14 guidelines. In the secondary sector the examination system dictates the curriculum from S3 upwards. In this context, if policymakers are not sympathetic to a curricular cause and if headteachers cannot create flexibility within their curriculum, minority areas such as GME will always struggle.

Gaelic, however, suffers a more substantial disadvantage. GME does not come within the portfolio of the Minister for Education and Young People but is the responsibility of the Minister for Arts and Cultural Heritage. In a world where GME is seen as one of factors which will impact upon the survival of the language, that simply does not make sense. That weakness has long been recognised by Gaelic organisations, for example CNAG, who have lobbied consistently for the situation to be changed. Educational commentators have also expressed the same view. Brown argues that 'there is an urgent priority for Gaelic Medium Education to become an explicit responsibility within the mainstream remit for education. Only then will its automatic consideration for funding become a part of the Executive's planning. Without that, there will continue to be a dependence on special cases being made as a result of urging by pressure groups' (Brown, 2002). The way that the ministerial portfolio with regard to Gaelic has developed does appear to be somewhat haphazard, often with an interested individual being given the brief, irrespective of how it fits with the other responsibilities within his/her portfolio. It is fair to say that civil servant support has been more consistent, however, coming mostly from those working within the Arts and Cultural Heritage section. The necessary link between language and culture is not one that can be denied. Certainly the Meek report has stressed that 'effective holistic planning requires synergy across and between all sectors including arts, media, community development and social and economic development. A well-organised and resourced programme of artistic and other out-of-school activities must support Gaelic-medium education' (Scottish Executive, 2002, p.25). However, where elements of educational policy-making are at stake, the validity of GME being only within the Arts and Cultural Heritage portfolio may be questioned.

In the consultation process leading to the Standards in Schools

(Scotland) Act of 2000 the Scottish Executive argued that the needs of GME would be better met in a Gaelic Language Act rather than in an Education Act. The attitude of the Gaelic world to that kind of thinking is well illustrated in the response of CNP. In a letter to the SNP's spokesperson on Education, Michael Russell, MSP, the Chairman of CNP, John Macleod, argues that 'Gaelic Medium Education is essentially an education service and its proper place is in an Education Bill. To leave legislative provision for Gaelic Medium Education to a Gaelic Language Bill sends out a message that Gaelic Medium Education is little more than a language support initiative. Gaelic Medium Education needs to be recognised as primarily an educationally beneficial service that should be within the national education sector of government'. (Macleod 2000).

The Scottish Executive did not respond positively to that plea. Instead it agreed that Gaelic and other lesser used languages should be included in its National Priorities for Education (Scottish Executive, 1999). For some, that represented a significant step forward insofar as it provided a statutory framework within which GME became a national educational priority. For others it was yet another lost opportunity to enshrine in law an entitlement to GME. That position is best illustrated by Robert Dunbar, then a Board Member of CNAG, in a letter to other Board Members. In his letter Dunbar writes: 'the designation of Gaelic as a "national priority" is both unnecessary, since there are no serious problems with the quality of existing provision, and irrelevant to the real issue, which is to ensure that parental demand is met. The designation of a matter as a "national priority does not . . . address the fundamental issue of a legal entitlement to Gaelic Medium Education"'. Dunbar goes on to suggest that a 'requirement on local authorities to set out objectives and to make an annual statement as to these objectives is completely inadequate. Indeed, he argues that to 'leave Gaelic wholly in the hands of local education authorities would be a disaster' (Dunbar, 2000). These comments from two critics are significant in highlighting three major issues which will affect the development of GME.

First, they allude to the strongly held belief in the Gaelic world that no substantial progress will be made either in GME or Gaelic as a whole without secure status for the language. CNAG has argued strongly that secure status or meaningful protection should be given to Gaelic through the passage of specific legislation. This, CNAG argues, 'should establish a basic principle of equal validity for Gaelic and English in Scotland along the lines of the recognition given to Welsh by virtue of the *Welsh Language Act 1993*' (CNAG, 1997). That secure status will have to be enshrined in statute, otherwise, it is argued, the language will never have the protection it needs to develop. The Gaelic language (Scotland) Bill was presented to the Scottish Parliament by Mike Russell of the SNP in

November 2002. Its main aim was to ensure that public bodies treat the Gaelic and English languages on an equal basis. However, checks would require to be put in place. Whereas the Official Languages Equality bill in Ireland of 2002 proposes an independent and dedicated Language Commissioner to oversee that the legislation is being fulfilled, the Gaelic Language Bill places powers of scrutiny in the hands of the Scottish Ombudsman.

Secondly, it is important to realise that these comments reflect a growing belief that GME should be an integral part of the educational system in Scotland. It should not remain so outwith the system that responsibility for it lies with another cabinet minister. The allocation of Specific Grants to GME (described in Chapters 1, 3, and 4,) simply reinforces the fact that it is different. It is funded and politically controlled in a way that is not aligned with the rest of the education system.

Thirdly, these comments point to a disappointment with the lack of support given by the local education authorities to GME. Notwithstanding the support of individuals within certain local authorities, there is no confidence that support will come from COSLA. That organisation's response to the 1997 consultation on the future development of Gaelic education was highly significant. When the then Education Minister, Brian Wilson, consulted on, among other issues, the duty of education authorities to provide Gaelic-medium primary education where a reasonable local demand existed, COSLA's response was quite clear. It reaffirmed its 'strong support for measures to support Gaelic and Gaelic-medium teaching' but opposed 'the imposition of a duty on local authorities to provide Gaelic Medium education'. (COSLA, 1997) The message could not be clearer. The local authorities as a whole in Scotland are not sympathetic to resourcing GME within their schools.

Shaping Future Contexts

GME has been one of the success stories of recent Scottish education. About 2,000 pupils are now involved in GME units and there has been a steady increase in uptake across the country. The latest figures from the University of Strathclyde suggest that the growth continues (University of Strathclyde, 2003). In session 2002–2003, 339 pupils enrolled in Primary 1 compared to 229 in the previous year. The transition from primary to secondary also shows encouraging signs of growth. A total of 149 of the 232 pupils (64%) who left primary school proceeded to GME at secondary level. The pressure on the secondary sector is illustrated by the fact that four additional secondary schools were obliged to provide GME in 2002–2003. Gaelic-medium units are securely established across Scotland. The evaluation of learning and teaching in these units has been very positive and pupils not only develop Gaelic language competence but also achieve at least the standards of their age group in the English-medium curriculum.

Much, however, still needs to be done, including a critical examination of how developments in the primary sector can be carried forward into secondary schools. That is an area which has been under-resourced as well as under-researched. In particular, the shortage of teachers, which is already a seemingly intractable problem in primary schools, could become even more critical in secondary schools if pupils educated in the primary sector continued to be educated through the medium of Gaelic at secondary level. Up until now that has not happened because provision has not normally been available in secondary schools. Nevertheless, the issue will have to be faced, when, for example, pupils begin to emerge from the Gaelic school in Glasgow to go to their designated secondary school.

The shortage of teachers will not be solved simply by changing the way that GME teachers are trained. A national recruitment strategy, aimed specifically at GME, will be a key requirement. Gaelic itself will need to have status as a language to attract both new recruits and existing teachers from other domains of the school curriculum. Teachers will have to feel secure that there is a career progression within GME. Above all, there will have to be confidence in the Gaelic community itself that there is and ought to be a future for its language, along with a belief across Scotland as a whole that, like the Scots language, it is a necessary element of a national culture, irrespective of whether or not it is relevant to the individual.

That is not to say that the professional training of teachers is unimportant. A new course, being introduced in September 2004, being prepared by the University of Strathclyde and the UHIMI, will, therefore, be of immense value. It will incorporate the recommendations of the 1999 GTCS report and will ensure that GME teachers will be trained through the medium of Gaelic.

There are, however, more fundamental issues to be resolved. It seems likely that GME will remain a peripheral educational issue until it comes within the remit of the Minister for Education and Young People. A step in that direction would, of course, have implications. It might, for example, mean the end of the Specific Grants. That may be a small price to pay if GME were to be funded and resourced in the same way as other parts of the education system. It would also challenge the commitment of some local authorities who have seen Specific Grants as another purse from which to spend on education in general rather on GME in particular.

There is no doubt that, given our present structure in Scotland, the relationship with the local authorities is critical. Local authorities jealously guard their responsibility for the stewardship of their schools. That is why we need a way of ensuring that local authorities meet identified criteria as far as GME planning is concerned. Questions relating to accountability need to be asked. Where, for example, does the role of HMIE lie? There is only one Gaelic HMIE in Scotland and he is a secondary school specialist. There is no Gaelic HMI in the primary sector where all the developments in GME of the past thirty years have taken place. That situation does not inspire confidence. There is a clear need for more Gaelic education professionals, in the same way as we need more representatives from other minority groups, in decision-making positions in Scotland.

Since the publication of the Macpherson Report (Scottish Executive, 2000) and the Meek Report (Scottish Executive, 2002) there is an assumption that the new Bòrd na Gaidhlig will solve many of these problems. It would be unsafe to make that assumption. The Bòrd will be financed directly by the Scottish Executive and that will leave it open to the charge that it is simply an agent of the very political system which is seen as inimical to GME development. It will have to be one of the Bòrd's main priorities to disabuse the Gaelic community of that thinking, but above all the Bòrd will have to impress upon people that it can be independent of government, that it can speak with an independent voice and that it can make recommendations that are not necessarily sympathetic to government thinking.

Almost as important will be the Bòrd's relationship with the local authorities. The history of the relationship between Comunn na Gàidhlig and the local authorities needs to be examined carefully to ensure that past tensions do not recur in the future. The Bòrd will need to work hard to reassure local authorities that it is not a threat to local democratic government, but is rather an agency that will support local authority initiatives to develop GME.

Despite these reservations, the progress made in the last twenty years creates a sense of optimism. Educationally exciting steps have been taken in the domain of GME in Scotland. Its growth has coincided with the emergence of a new parliament in Scotland. As they mature, both the Gaelic world and the Scottish Parliament must understand that positive dialogue is the only way forward. They will also need to understand that old solutions will not fit new challenges.

In a monolingual country it is sometimes difficult to alert ourselves to the power and potential of language. Language, after all, is the vehicle of traditional values. It is the basis for self respect and the basis of a sense of belonging. It is the tool for creative thought, of constructive question formulation and problem-solving. A child's mother tongue therefore is not something that should be cast aside when s/he reaches school age. His/her mother tongue 'is part of the stuff of which his mind is built; it embodies the ideas and attitudes he has gained from his environment; it is the language through which he has acquired the earliest experiences of life; and it is the language by which he dreams, thinks, cherishes, loves, scolds and learns' (Bambgose, 1976, p.34). Few would disagree with David Crystal's observation that language is also 'the most immediate and universal symbol of identity' (Crystal, 1997, p.115). Yet in Scotland we have maintained a rather awkward relationship with language, and will continue to do so if it is not accepted as a necessary element of who we are. According to census data, the number of speakers of Gaelic has fallen from 65,978 in 1991 to 58,650 in 2001. If Gaelic as a language is to survive into the next century, a daunting task in the global village, then GME will require attention as one of several key language planning factors central to the survival policy.

REFERENCES

Aitchison, J, and Carter, H, (2000), *Language, Economy and Society: The Changing Fortunes of the Welsh Language in the Twentieth Century*, University of Wales Press, Cardiff.

Andrews, Liam, (1997), '*The very dogs in Belfast will bark in Irish*: The Unionist Government and the Irish language 1921–43', in *The Irish Language in Northern Ireland*, ed. by Aodán Mac Póilin, pp.49–94. Iontaobhas ULTACH / ULTACH Trust, Belfast.

Azurmendi, M-J, et al., (2001), 'Reversing Language Shift: The Case of Basque', in *Can Threatened Languages Be Saved? Reversing Language Shift, Revisited: A 21st Century Perspective*, ed. by Joshua A. Fishman, pp.234–59, Multilingual Matters, Cleveden.

Baker, C, (1993), 'Bilingual Education in Wales', in *European Models of Bilingual Education*, ed. by Hugo Baetens Beardsmore, pp.7–29, Multilingual Matters, Cleveden.

Baker, C, (1993), *Foundations of Bilingual Education and Bilingualism*, Multilingual Matters, Cleveden.

Baker, C, (1996), *A Parents' and Teachers' Guide to Bilingualism*, Multilingual Matters, Clevedon.

Baker, C, and Prys Jones, M, (2000), 'Welsh Language Education: A Strategy for Revitalization', in Williams (2000), pp.116–37.

Bambgose, A (Ed), (1976), *Mother tongue education the West African experience*, Hodder and Stoughton, London.

Brown, S, (2002), Teacher Education for Gaelic-Medium Teaching, Internal report to UHMI, commissioned by Sabhal Mor Ostaig.

Buchanan, J, (2002), 'The Gaelic Communities', in *Anatomy of the New Scotland*, ed. by Hassan, G, and Warhurst, C, pp.270–76, Mainstream Publishing, Edinburgh.

Census of Scotland, (1981, 1991, 2001), General Register Office, Edinburgh

CNAG, (1997), Inbhe Thearainte Dhan Ghaidlig, CNAG, Inverness, 1997.

Coimisiún na Gaeltachta, (2002), *Tuarascáil/Report*. Dub. Coimisiún na

Gaeltachta, Dublin.

Comhairle nan Eilean Siar, (1996), *Leirmheas buileachaidh Poileasaidh Foghlaim Dà-Chànanach / Bilingual Education Policy Implementation Review*, Comhairle nan Eilean Siar, Stornoway.

Comhar na Múinteoirí Gaeilge, (2003), *Bróisiúr Eolais: Cursaí Gaeilge ag an Tríú Leibhéal*, Comhar na Múinteoirí Gaeilge, Dublin.

COSLA, (1997), Letter to SEED

Crystal, D, (1997), English as a Global Language, CUP, Cambridge.

Dunbar, R, (2000), Letter to fellow Board members of CNAG, 1 June.

Edwards, J, (1985), *Language, Society and Identity*, Blackwell.

Etxeberria Balerdi, F, (2002), 'New Challenges of the Bilingual Education in the Basque Country' (paper published on-line at *http://www.eblul.org/ BILINGUISMOENGLISH.doc*).

Evans, W, Gareth, (2000), 'The British State and Welsh-Language Education 1914–1991', in *'Let's Do Our Best for the Ancient Tongue'*: *The Welsh Language in the Twentieth Century*, ed. by G H Jenkins and M A Williams, pp.343–69. University of Wales Press, Cardiff.

Ferguson, M, (2002), letter to *Edinburgh Evening News* of 17 April.

Fishman, J, (1991), *Reversing Language Shift: Theoretical and Empirical Foundations of Assistance to Threatened Languages*, Multilingual Matters, Cleveden.

Gardner, Nicholas, (2001), *'Language Policy for Education in the Basque Country'*. Paper presented at Comunn na Gàidhlig's Còmhdhail 2001, Edinburgh, June 12 (available on-line at *www.cnag.org.uk/ basque.htm*)

Gardner, Nicholas, (2002), *Basque in Education in the Basque Autonomous Community*. Vitoria-Gasteiz: Eusko Jaurlaritza / Gobierno Vasco.

General Teaching Council for Scotland, (1999), *Teagasg ann am Foghlam tro Mheadhan na Gàidhlig: Molaidhean Leasachaidh / Teaching in Gaelic Medium Education: Recommendations for change*, GTC(S), Edinburgh.

Grant, N, (2000), *Multicultural Education in Scotland*, Dunedin Academic Press, Edinburgh.

Gruffudd, H, (1999), 'Education and first language use'. Paper presented at the Seventh International Conference on Minority Languages, Bilbao, 1–3 December.

Gruffudd, H, (2000), 'Planning for the Use of Welsh by Young People', in Williams 2000, pp.173–207.

Hickey, T, (1997), *Early Immersion Education in Ireland: Na Naionrai*, Institiuid Teangeolaiochta Eireann, Dublin.

Highland Council, (2000), Gaelic Medium Education: Language Guidelines, HMI Report, Inverness

Hindley, R, (1991), *The Death of the Irish Language: A Qualified Obituary*. Routledge, London.

Committee of Enquiry into the Functions and Powers of the Islands Councils of Scotland, (1984), Chairman Sir David Montgomery, HMSO, (out of print)

Johnstone, R, Harlen, W, MacNeil, M, Stradling, R and Thorpe, G, (1999) *The Attainment of Pupils Receiving Gaelic Medium Education in Scotland*, Scottish CILT on behalf of the Scottish Executive Education Department, Stirling (summary available online at: *http://www.scotland.gov.uk/library3/education/i62-02.asp*).

Kemp, J, 'Do not follow the Irish Gaelic example' in *The Herald*, 3 May 2002

Kirk, J, and D P Ó Baoill, eds. (2001), *Linguistic Politics: Language Policies for Northern Ireland, the Republic of Ireland, and Scotland*, Cló Ollscoil na Ríona, Belfast.

Kirk, J M, and D P Ó Baoill, eds. (2002). *Language Planning and Education: Linguistic Issues in Northern Ireland, the Republic of Ireland, and Scotland*, Cló Ollscoil na Ríona, Belfast.

Lapkin, S, (1990), 'French Immersion Research Agenda for the '90s', *Canadian Modern Language Review*, 46.

Lasagabaster, D, (2001), 'Bilingualism, Immersion Programmes and Language Learning in the Basque Country', *Journal of Multilingual and Multicultural Development*, 22, 401–25.

MacCaluim, A, (2002), 'Periphery of the Periphery? Adult Learners of Scottish Gaelic and Reversal of Language Shift', unpublished PhD thesis, University of Edinburgh.

McCoy, G, (2001), 'From Cause to Quango?: The Peace Process and the Transformation of the Irish Language Movement', in Kirk and Ó Baoill, (2001), pp.205–18.

MacDonald, S, (1997), *Reimagining Culture: Histories, Identities and the Gaelic Renaissance*, Berg, Oxford.

MacKinnon, K, (1994), *Gaelic in 1994*, Report to the Euromosaic Project, Black Isle.

MacKinnon, K, (1995), 'The Dynamics of Scottish Gaelic'. Paper presented at the conference on Language Policy and Planning in the European Union, University of Liverpool, 28–29 April [abbreviated version published in *Watching One's Tongue: Aspects of Romance and Celtic Languages*, ed. by Nic Craith, M, pp.177–200, Liverpool University Press, Liverpool.

MacLeod, J, (2000), letter to Mike Russell, of 17 April.

MacLeod, M, (1966), 'Gaelic in Highland Education' in *Transactions of the Gaelic Society of Inverness*, Vol. XLIII, pp.305–334

McLeod, W, (2001), 'Gaelic in the New Scotland: Politics, Rhetoric, and Public Discourse', *Journal on Ethnopolitics and Minority Issues in Europe* (available on the Internet at *http://www.ecmi.de/jemie/download/JEMIE02MacLeod28-11-01.pdf*).

McLeod, W, and Dunbar, R, (forthcoming). 'Foghlam tro Mheadhan na

Gàidhlig ann an Alba / Gaelic-Medium Education in Scotland', in *Gaelic-medium Education: Provision in Northern Ireland, Scotland, the Republic of Ireland and the Isle of Man*, ed. by Scott, M, and Ní Bhaoill, R, Cló Ollscoil na Banríona, Belfast.

MacNamara, J, (1966), *Bilingualism and Primary Education: A Study of Irish Experience*, Edinburgh University Press, Edinburgh.

Mac Póilin, A, (1997), 'Aspects of the Irish language movement', in *The Irish Language in Northern Ireland*, ed. by Aodán Mac Póilin, pp.171–89, Iontaobhas ULTACH / ULTACH Trust, Belfast.

Mac Póilin, A, (2000), 'Taig Talk', in *Aithne na nGael /Gaelic Identities*, ed. by Gordon McCoy with Maolcholaim Scott, pp.88–95, Institute of Irish Studies, Queen's University Belfast / ULTACH Trust, Belfast.

Maguire, G, (1991), *Our Own Language: An Irish Initiative*, Multilingual Matters, Cleveden.

Mercator-Education, (1997), *The Irish language in education in Northern Ireland* [authored by Mac Póilin, A,] Mercator-Education, Leeuwarden, Netherlands.

Mercator-Education, (1998), *The Basque language in education in France* [authored by Stuijt, M, et al.] Mercator-Education, Leeuwarden, Netherlands.

Mercator-Education, (2000), *The Basque language in education in Spain* [authored by Gardner, N,] Mercator-Education, Leeuwarden, Netherlands.

Mercator-Education, (2001), *The Irish language in education in the Republic of Ireland* [authored by Ó Murchú, H,] Mercator-Education, Leeuwarden, Netherlands.

Mercator-Education, (2001), *The Gaelic language in education in the UK* [authored by Robertson, B,] Mercator-Education, Leeuwarden, Netherlands.

Mercator-Education, (2001), *The Welsh language in education in the UK* [authored by Jones, M,] Mercator-Education, Leeuwarden, Netherlands.

Morris, S, (2000), 'Adult Education, Language Revival and Language Planning', in Williams, (2000), pp.208–220.

Murray, J, and Morrison, C, (1984), *Bilingual Primary Education*, Acair, Stornoway.

Ní Fhearghusa, J, (2000), 'The Importance of Independent Dedicated Irish-Medium Schools', in *Sgoil Ghàidhlig airson Baile Dhùn Èideann: Latha Fiosrachaidh / A Gaelic-Medium School for Edinburgh: Information Day*, 29–33. Comann nam Pàrant, Edinburgh (Dùn Èideann agus Lodainn).

Ní Fhearghusa, J, (2002), 'Structúir Éagsúla an Ghaeloideachais', in Kirk and Ó Baoill (2002) pp.43–51.

Nicolson, A, (1867), 'Report on the State of Eucation in the Hebrides' in Parliamentary Papers, Vol XXV

Nicolson, M, (2000), 'Language Learners and Diverse Legacies: Question of Confidence' in *Scottish Educational Review, Vol 32, No 2*.

Nicolson, M, (forthcoming), *Language and who we are: some Scottish HE student perspectives*, being prepared for publication.

Nig Uidhir, G, (2002), 'Initial Teacher Training for Irish-Medium Schools', in Kirk and Ó Baoill (2002), pp.65–75.

Ó Baoill, D, (1999), 'Social cultural distance, integrational orientation and the learning of Irish', in *Intercultural Communication and Language Learning*, ed. by Chambers, A and Ó Baoill, D, pp.189–200, Irish Association for Applied Linguistics / Royal Irish Academy, Dublin.

Ó Huallacháin, C, (1994), *The Irish and Irish — a sociolinguistic analysis of the relationship between a people and their language*, Irish Franciscan Provincial Office, Dublin.

Ó Laoire, M, (2002), 'An Ghaeilge sa Chóras Oideachais: Polasaí Pleanáil agus Teagasc', *Léachtaí Cholm Cille XXXII (Curaclam na Gaeilge)*, pp.74–104.

Ó Murchú, M, (2002), *Cás na Gaeilge 1952–2002: Ag Dul ó Chion?* An Aimsir Óg Paimfléad 1. Coiscéim, Dublin.

Ó Murchudha, N, (2001), *Staid Reatha na Gaeilge mar Mheán Cumarsáid sna Limistéir Ghaeltachta: Tuaracáil do Chomisiún na Gaeltachta*, Comisiún na Gaeltachta, Dublin.

Ó Riagáin, P, (1997), *Language Policy and Social Reproduction: Ireland 1893–1993*, Clarendon Press, Oxford.

Ó Riagáin, P, (2001), 'Irish Language Production and Reproduction 1981–1996', in *Can Threatened Languages Be Saved? Reversing Language Shift, Revisited: A 21st Century Perspective*, ed. by Fishman, J.A, pp.195–214, Multilingual Matters, Cleveden.

Peover, S, (2001), 'Encouragement and Facilitation: A New Paradigm for Minority Language Education', in Kirk and Ó Baoill (2001), pp.195–204.

Peover, S, (2002), 'The Current State of Irish-Medium Education in Northern Ireland', in Kirk and Ó Baoill 2002, pp.124–30.

Reynolds, D, et al., (1998), *A Competitive Edge: Why Welsh Medium Schools Perform Better*, Institute of Welsh Affairs, Cardiff.

Scottish Executive, (1997), *National Priorities in Education* — HMSO — available online at: *http://www.scotland.gov.uk/education/national-priorities/default.asp*.

Scottish Executive, (1999 and 2000), Improving our Schools, available online at *www.scotland.gov.uk/improvingschools/*

Scottish Executive, (2000), *Gaelic: Revitalising Gaelic, a National Asset*, Chairman, John Alick MacPherson, available online at: *http://www.scotland.gov.uk/library/3/heritage/gtfr-02.asp_b*

Scottish Executive, (2002), *Report of the Ministerial Advisory Group on Gaelic*, Chairman Donald Meek, HMSO, executive summary available

References 79

Scottish Office Education Department, (1965), *Primary Education in Scotland*, HMSO.
Scottish Office Education Department, (1993), *National Guidelines for Curriculum and Assessment in Scotland: Gaelic 5–14*
Scottish Office Education Department, (1994), *Provision for Gaelic Education in Scotland: A Report by HM Inspectors of Schools*.
SSPCK records GD95/1–14 can be consulted at General Register House, Edinburgh.
Stradling, R, and MacNeil, M, (1995), *Teacher Training for Gaelic Medium Education*, Leirsinn Research Centre, Isle of Skye.
Stradling, R, and MacNeil, M, (1996), *Gaelic Medium Education: The Critical Skills*, Leirsinn Research Centre, Isle of Skye, on behalf of the Inter-Authority Standing Group for Gaelic.
Stradling, R, and MacNeil, M, (1999), *Emergent Identities and Bilingual Education: The Teenage Years*, Leirsinn Research Centre, Isle of Skye on behalf of the Management Review Group.
Stradling, R, and MacNeil, M, (2000), Home and Community: *Their role in enhancing the Gaelic language competencies of children in Gaelic Medium Education*, Leirsinn Research Centre, Isle of Skye.
The Highland Council, (2000), *Gaelic Medium Education: Language Guidelines*, Inverness HMI Report.
Thomas, W P, and Collier, V P, (1997), *School Effectiveness for Language Minority Students*, National Clearinghouse for Bilingual Education, Washington, DC, available online at: *http://www.ncbe.gwu.edu/ncbepubs/resource/effectiveness/index.htm*
University of Strathclyde, (2003), *Number of Pupils in Gaelic Medium Education*.
Withers, C.W.J. (1998), *Urban Highlanders*, Tuckwell Press, East Linton.
Walsh, J, ed., (forthcoming). *Ollscolaíocht Ghaeilge: Dúshláin agus Léargais / University Education in Irish: Challenges and Perspectives*. FIONTAR, Dublin City University, Dublin.
Williams, C H, ed. (2000), *Language Revitalization: Policy and Planning in Wales*, University of Wales Press, Cardiff.
Wyn Jones, R, et al. (2002), 'Keeping Up Appearances: Welsh-Language Provision in Higher Education', *Planet*, 154, pp.7–15.